LONDON'S SMALLER BUS TYPES SINCE 1986

DAVID BEDDALL

PEN & SWORD
TRANSPORT
AN IMPRINT OF PEN & SWORD BOOKS LTD.
YORKSHIRE – PHILADELPHIA

First published in Great Britain in 2026
Pen & Sword Transport
An imprint of
Pen & Sword Books Ltd
Yorkshire – Philadelphia

ISBN 978 1 03610 965 3

A CIP catalogue record for this book is available from the British Library.

Typeset in 12/16 Palatino by SJmagic DESIGN SERVICES, India.

Printed and bound in India by Replika Press Pvt. Ltd.

The Publisher's authorised representative in the EU for product safety is Authorised Rep Compliance Ltd., Ground Floor, 71 Lower Baggot Street, Dublin D02 P593, Ireland.
www.arccompliance.com

For a complete list of Pen & Sword titles please contact

PEN & SWORD BOOKS LIMITED
George House, Beevor Street, Off Pontefract Road, Hoyle Mill, Barnsley, South Yorkshire, England, S71 1HN.
E-mail: enquiries@pen-and-sword.co.uk
Website: www.pen-and-sword.co.uk

or

PEN AND SWORD BOOKS
1950 Lawrence Road, Havertown, PA 19083, USA
E-mail: uspen-and-sword@casematepublishers.com
Website: www.penandswordbooks.com

FSC
www.fsc.org
MIX
Paper | Supporting responsible forestry
FSC™ C016779

LONDON'S SMALLER BUS TYPES SINCE 1986

Dedicated to the memory of Jonathan Spencer,
a truly inspirational man

CONTENTS

ACKNOWLEDGEMENTS

I would like to thank my wife, Helen, and my two sons, Morris and Matthew, for their continued patience whilst producing this book. My sincere thanks go to both Liam Farrer-Beddall and Gary Seamarks for allowing me to use photographs from their collections, and for also taking the time to read through the draft of this book. I would also like to thank Ben Everitt, Ian Armstrong, Mike Harris, Phil Hambling and David Haig for allowing me to use their photographs.

INTRODUCTION

London has always had a number of standard vehicle types, dating back to the B-type introduced by the London General Omnibus Company in the 1900s. The London Passenger Transport Board, later London Transport, were keen to have standard types of vehicles operating their services, from the AEC Regent RT, RTL and RTW types, the Routemasters of the 1950s and 1960s, to the Leyland Fleetlines, AEC Merlins, Leyland Swifts, Leyland Nationals, MCW Metrobuses and Leyland Titans of the 1970s and 1980s.

However, the amalgamation of a number of independents into London General and London Transport also saw a number of smaller varying types of buses operated by these large operators. Many of these were eradicated due to London Transport standardising their fleet. London Transport began to introduce other smaller types of buses during the 1970s to try to find replacements for certain, unpopular types.

Under the guise of London Buses Limited, a range of different types of buses and coaches were purchased or leased by the company to operate their services. Whilst the privatised companies post 1994 had a tendency to stick with a standard type, there were a number of much smaller batches of buses that were operated by these new operators.

London's Smaller Bus Types Since 1986 takes a look at the history of the fleet of non-standard diesel and hybrid buses that were taken into stock by London's bus operators from that date. The book concludes with a look at the various coaches that were operated by these privatised operators. This book is up to date to July 2025.

David Beddall
Rushden, August 2025

VOLVO AILSA

LONDON TRANSPORT/LONDON BUSES LIMITED

By 1984 London Transport were receiving a number of Leyland Titans and MCW Metrobuses. At the same time, London Transport were looking at undertaking trials of a number of different types in readiness for the next generation of buses. Amongst these were three Volvo Ailsa B55 buses, allowing London Transport to evaluate a front-engined vehicle.

The first pair, V1 and V2 (A101/2SUU), arrived in April 1984 carrying Alexander R bodywork, introducing this body manufacturer to London Transport. The pair were allocated to Stockwell along with other trial vehicles. They were put to use on the 170 (Clapham Junction–Wandsworth–Putney Heath–Roehampton), with appearances on the 44 (Tooting Station–Tooting Broadway–Wansdworth–Battersea–Vauxhall Station) on Sundays.

They were joined in March 1985 by V3 (A103SUU). Carrying a similar body to the first two, V3 featured a second door at the rear rather than the centre and had two staircases. The twin staircase meant that V3 had to be crew-operated rather than a one-person-operated vehicle. It was initially used on the 77A (Aldwych–Wandsworth), later being used on the 88 between Oxford Circus and Clapham Common.

V1 to V3 were reallocated to Potters Bar in February 1987, where they received broad white bands and a black skirt. At this time Potters Bar garage became home to one of several low-cost units introduced by London Buses Limited. V1-3 were joined there by thirteen similar Van Hool McArdle bodied Ailsas which had been acquired by London Buses from South Yorkshire PTE. One of these, LWB378P, was acquired and was allocated stock number V15, but was withdrawn and used for spare parts. The others carried registration marks LWB389, 408/9, 375, 394P, NAK412/3/6/20R, LWB369/77/87P and were numbered V4-14/6. V16 was renumbered in June 1987 to V15, replacing the one acquired for spare parts. V4-14 were taken into stock during March, with V15 and V16 arriving in April. Standard red livery was applied to these buses, along with the wide white band and black skirts. They were used on routes 84 (St Albans–New Barnet Station); 234 (East Finchley Station–Barnet); 242 (Waltham Abbey–Potters Bar); 263 (Archway Station–Barnet Hospital); 310A (Enfield Town–Hertford) and W8 (Picketts Lock Centre–Chase Farm Hospital).

These were followed by another fifty Volvo Ailsas which had been acquired from West Midlands PTE. Carrying Alexander AV bodywork these buses were numbered V16 to V65 by London Buses Limited. Registration marks JOV766-787, 738-765P were carried by these buses. Delivery of these double-deckers was drawn out, starting in July 1987 and being completed in March 1988. V25/7/9, 30/8/9, 49, 52/4/5/7, 65 were first to arrive, doing so in July 1987. These were followed by V16-9, 22/3/6/8, 32/3/7, 42/7, 58, 60-3 in August. V35-6, 44-6/8 arrived in September with V21, 40/1/3, 50/6, 64 appearing in October. Two more, V53 and V59, entered the fleet in November. V24, 31 and 51 arrived in December. V20 completed the batch when it arrived in March 1988. V16 V17/9, 22/3/5-30/2/9, 42/7/9, 52/4/5/7, 63/5 joined V1-15 at Potters Bar, whilst V18, 20/1/4, 31/3-8, 40/1/3-6/8, 50/1/3/6/8-62/4 were allocated to Harrow Weald for use with the new low-cost Harrow Buses operation. These saw service on the 114 between Mill Hill Broadway and Ruislip, via South Harrow; the 140 (Heathrow Airport–Harrow–Harrow Weald); 183 (Golders Green–Harrow–Pinner) and the 340 running between Edgware Station and Harrow. A red and cream livery was worn by those allocated to Harrow Weald, with prominent Harrow Buses fleet names. The second-hand Ailsas had a short career in London, with the type being withdrawn and sold between October 1989 and February 1991. Many of the type saw further service with independent operator Black Prince of Morley, West Yorkshire.

V1 and V2 lasted much longer than their second-hand counterparts. They continued to be used from Potters Bar, surviving privatisation, passing to MTL London Northern at this time. In June 1995 the pair passed to London Suburban Bus, being used on the 4 (Archway Station–Islington Angel–Waterloo), before eventually leaving London in November 1995, passing to MTL Liverpool.

V3, however, had its career in London cut short in November 1992 when it was involved in an accident with a tree. It was due to be scrapped but was saved by Black Prince who rebuilt the bus.

BORO'LINE

Boro'line of Maidstone was the only other operator of the Volvo Ailsa in the Greater London area. The company gained the contracts for LRT routes 422 (Bexleyheath–Woolwich High Street) and 492 (Sidcup Station–Dartford) in November 1988 at the expense of

V3 (A103SUU) was new in March 1985 and featured a twin staircase. It is seen blinded for route 107 to Queensbury Station. *Ian Armstrong Collection*

1985 saw the arrival of a sizable batch of Volvo Ailsas from both West Midlands and South Yorkshire PTE. V21 (JOV771P) was a former West Midlands example and was allocated to the Harrow Buses operation. It is seen at Heathrow Central Bus station before heading back to Harrow Weald. *Ian Armstrong Collection*

Bexleybus. Initially operated by a fleet of hired Leyland Nationals from London Country North East, Boro'line purchased four Leyland Nationals and eight Alexander AV bodied Volvo Ailsas, the latter being purchased from Ensign Bus, formerly operating with Tayside. These were numbered 911-8 (LES48P, NSP313-6/8/9/22R). They wore the distinctive blue and yellow, with a silver-grey skirt livery.

V48 (JOV748P) was another former West Midlands PTE Ailsa allocated to the Harrow Buses operation. It is seen passing Harrow bus station on its way to Northolt on route 140. *Ian Armstrong Collection*

DENNIS DOMINATOR

LONDON BUSES LIMITED

The Dennis Dominator was another type used in the alternative vehicle evaluations. Three were taken into stock by London Transport carrying Northern Counties bodywork. Numbered H1 to H3 (B101-3WUW) they were taken into stock in November 1984. London Buses Limited took them on in April 1985. They were added to Stockwell's allocation where they were used on the 170 (Roehampton–Clapham Junction–Vauxhall–Aldwych). The

H3 (B103WUW) is seen departing Crystal Palace at the start of its journey to Oxford Circus on the 137. *Ian Armstrong Collection*

trial finished in August 1986, at which time they were put into storage at Merton. H1-3 found a new home at Brixton in June 1987 where they were used on the 137 (Crystal Palace–Oxford Circus–Archway), working on Sundays on the 159 (West Hampstead–Streatham, Green Lane) from January 1990. Ownership passed to London Coaches at Wandsworth in October 1991, being privatised with this operation in May 1992. H2 and H3 were repainted into London Pride white and red livery, whilst H1 was withdrawn in December 1992. H2 and H3 passed to Capital Citybus in August 1993, remaining with them when the company was acquired by First Group. No further orders for the Dominator were placed by London Buses Limited.

LONDON COUNTRY

London Country South West purchased nine Dennis Dominators, the first arriving in 1988, it being fitted with an East Lancs body. Registered F201OPD it was given fleet number DD1 when it arrived in December. Fitted with coach seats it was intended to operate on coach work. However, allocated to Leatherhead, it was used on the 408 between Guildford and Croydon. This bus was renumbered 601 in early 1989. It was then allocated to Green Line service 715, which later became the 415 (Guildford–London Victoria).

Eight more Dennis Dominators entered the London & Country fleet in spring 1989, these again carrying East Lancs bodywork. Seven of these were built to H45/31F specification and put to use on the 131 (Weybridge–Kingston), displacing older Leyland Atlanteans. The eighth was slightly longer, being built to a H49/35F specification. They followed on as 602 to 609 (F602-9RPG) and wore the new two-tone green livery. 602-8 were initially allocated to Weybridge for the 131, but new Volvos were introduced at Weybridge in April resulting in the transfer of these buses to Leatherhead in September, operating

Nine East Lancs bodied Dennis Dominators were taken into stock by London Country South West and London & Country in 1988/1989. The last of these was numbered 609 (F609RPG) which is seen loading in Eden Street, Kingston. *Ian Armstrong Collection*

its workings on the 131. London & Country lost the 131 to Westlink in September 1990, the Dominators finding other work. During 1992 they were put to use on the 57 between Streatham Hill and Kingston, working alongside Leyland Olympians. Fleet numbers DD2 to DD9 were allocated to these buses in January 1996 after the acquisition of other Dominators. Withdrawal took place in May 1998, with the eight double-deckers being sold for further use.

ENSIGN BUS/CAPITAL CITYBUS

By the end of 1989 Ensign Bus was operating LRT contracts in the Barking, Upminster and Romford area of north-east London. Using a fleet of second-hand buses, Ensign realized that in order to expand the business they would need to invest in new rolling stock. The company ordered twenty-four dual-door Northern Counties bodied Dennis Dominators. A demonstrator was loaned from Ipswich Buses in November 1989 to familiarise the engineering staff with the new model. Fleet numbers 251 to 274 were allotted to these buses which carried registration marks H251-9, 460, 261-74KVX. First to be delivered was 256, arriving in October 1990. Two months later, Ensign sold its operations to Hong Kong based CNT Group in December. The remaining twenty-three Dominators, arriving in January 1991, were therefore delivered to the new owners who initially used the Ensign Citybus name. They wore the blue and silver livery, replacing second-hand buses on the 62, 62A (Barking–Little Heath) and 248 (Romford–Cranham). Purfleet was the original base for the operations. The distinctive yellow with red lines livery was quickly adopted, along with the Capital Citybus fleet name. Following the collapse of the London Forest operation in November 1991, twelve of these Dominators were repainted yellow in preparation to take over services in the Walthamstow area, these twelve being made available after the loss of the 62 and 62A. They were re-allocated to Northumberland Park for use on the 97 (Chingford–Leyton).

Two more Dominators arrived in October 1991, allocated to Northumberland Park. These single-doored buses were registered J181/2HME, being numbered 181 and 182 by the company. They wore the distinctive yellow livery and were put to use on routes 97A (Chingford Station–Walthamstow Central) and 215 (Walthamstow Central–Lea Valley Campsite), working alongside Leyland Olympians.

Eight East Lancs bodied Dennis Dominators were acquired by Capital Citybus in October 1992 from Southampton Citybus, using them on the newly won route 257 (Stratford–Walthamstow Central). Registered F291-8PTP, these buses were numbered 191 to 198 by Capital Citybus. These were also allocated to Northumberland Park.

As mentioned above under the London Buses Limited heading, B102/3WUW were acquired by Capital Citybus in August 1993, having operated with London Coaches in between their time with London Buses and Capital Citybus. They were repainted yellow and worked from all three Citybus garages at Northumberland Park, Dagenham and Barking as required. 202 was de-roofed when it hit a bridge in Cranham in November 1996, but was repaired. They soldiered on in service until November 1999 when they moved north to First Leicester.

Three Alexander RH bodied Dominators were acquired from South Yorkshire Transport in October 1994. Registered B440/3/4CKW they were numbered 190, 183 and 184. Originally allocated to Northumberland Park, they made the move to Dagenham in July 1995 where they remained until March 1998, at which time they found a new home at Hackney. Withdrawal came at the end of 1999, beginning of 2000.

Another eight Alexander RH bodied Dominators arrived in March 1995 from Kelvin Central. At this time, the East London line was undergoing a refurbishment resulting in the closure of the line. These buses were used on one of the East London Line rail replacement contracts. These were repainted in an orange and white livery for the route, running between New Cross Gate and Aldgate. Numbered 185-9, 199-201/4, these carried registration marks DEM83X, CHF346-9/53/50/1X and DEM84X. The route was initially operated from Northumberland Park before transferring to Hackney in October 1996.

The early part of 1996 saw some routes in the Romford area re-acquired by Capital Citybus, resulting in the need for more buses. To help with this, seven second-hand Dennis Dominators bodied by East Lancs were acquired from Leicester Citybus in April 1996. Rolling stock numbers 340-2/4/5/7/8 (F140-2/4/5/7/8MBC) were allocated to these buses. Allocated to Dagenham, they were used on the 248, as well as the 165 (Romford Market–Rainham, Abbey Wood Lane) and 365 (Mardyke Estate–Havering Park).

181 and 182 transferred to Hackney garage in October 1996. From there they worked routes D6 (Hackney Central–Crossharbour) and 257 (Stratford–Walthamstow Central).

268 and 274 (H268/74KVX) gained the red and yellow livery early in 1997 when they were used on the 91 between Crouch End Broadway and Trafalgar Square. They were used to cover for the late arrival of Volvo Olympians.

The demise of the Dominator started in 2000 when members of the 191 to 198 and the 340-2/4/5/7/8 batches left London for pastures new. The last of these had gone by the summer of 2001. The majority of the original fleet of Dominators (251-74) remained in service until March 2002, when they were withdrawn and sold. Some were retained until September for use on rail replacement work from Rainham. 181 and 182 held on until the end of 2002, beginning of 2003, when they joined other former Capital Citybus Dominators at First Glasgow.

LONDON PRIDE

The London Pride Sightseeing operation was owned by Ensign Bus and used a number of second-hand Dennis Dominators. The first pair arrived in September 1993 when B103/5UAT were acquired from Kingston-Upon-Hull. These Alexander RH bodied examples were numbered 103 and 105 respectively and remained fully closed.

The next two Dominators arrived in 1995, this time being acquired from Swindon based Thamesdown Transport. Carrying Northern Counties bodywork, these were numbered 106 and 107 (SMW57/8Y), again remaining fully enclosed.

Seven East Lancs bodied Dennis Dominators were taken into stock in 1994, originating with Eastbourne Buses. Four arrived in April registered FDY142-5X, these taking up stock numbers 242/3, 344 and 245. 346 (FDY146X) followed in May. 238 and 339 (MPN138/9W) were last to arrive in September. 339, 344 and 346 became fully open-top buses, whilst 238/42/3/5 were rebuilt to part open-top layout. 242/3/5 were retained until after the acquisition of the business by Arriva in March 2001.

261 (H261KXV) was new to Ensign Bus in October 1990. January 1991 saw the batch transfer to the ownership of the CNT Group, becoming Ensign Citybus, later Capital Citybus. It is seen on its way to Collier Row whilst operating the 252. *Michael Whitingham/David Beddall Collection*

Eight Dominators originating with Cleveland Transit were taken into stock in November 1998, these carrying Northern Counties bodywork. Four of these were built to part open-top layout, taking up fleet numbers 200 to 203 (GAJ200/1V, VVN202/3Y). The other four carried registration marks A204-7EHN, being numbered 304 to 307 by London Pride, these being converted to full open-top. All were single-doored double-deckers. 202 and 203 were the only members of the eight to be acquired by Arriva The Original London Sightseeing Tour (TOLST) in October 2001. They lasted with their new owners until 2005.

The final Dominators to be taken into stock by London Pride arrived from Kelvin Central in June 1995. These were converted to part-open top specification. Registered FGE430/9X, TYS265W and MNS45Y they gained fleet numbers 230 to 233. The first and last members survived until the TOLST take over.

Romford Station finds 184 (B444CKW), one of four Alexander RH bodied Dennis Dominators acquired from South Yorkshire PTE in October 1994. *Ian Armstrong Collection*

In 1996 seven Dennis Dominators arrived from Leicester Citybus to help cover routes in the Romford area. 347 (F147MBC) represents this batch. *Ian Armstrong Collection*

VOLVO CITYBUS

Volvo produced the Citybus model from the mid-1980s, and was introduced to compete with the Leyland Olympian and Scania double-deck models. It was based on the B10M coach chassis. Bodied by East Lancs, Northern Counties and Alexander, a number of Volvo Citybuses were purchased by various operators in the London area for use on LRT contracts.

LONDON BUSES LIMITED

The first Volvo Citybus was delivered to London Buses Limited in August 1985 registered C101CUL, taking fleet number C1. This was a one-off vehicle, a Volvo Cumulo Citybus model leased for a three-year period as part of the alternative vehicle evaluation trial. Featuring an under-floor engine, the double-decker carried an Alexander R body similar to that of Volvo Ailsas V1 and V2. Although it arrived in the summer of 1985, it did not enter service until July 1986, doing so on the 102 (Golders Green–Chingford Station) from Palmers Green garage. It was returned to the Kirkby Plaxton Group in September 1987, at which time it had its Cumulo gear system replaced by a standard gearbox. It later saw service with A1 Services and Black Prince of Morley.

Twenty-seven Northern Counties bodied Volvo B10M Citybuses were purchased by London Buses Limited during 1989 for use on route 133 (Liverpool Street–Tooting Broadway). These dual-door buses featured a central staircase and split-level step entrances. They were allocated to London General's Stockwell garage wearing a red livery complete with a grey skirt. These took up rolling stock numbers VC1 to VC27 (G101-27NGN). VC1-3/7-14 arrived in

November, VC4-6/15-23/5-7 in December and VC24 in January 1990. Coach seats were fitted to VC1-3 on both decks, whilst VC4-6 featured them on the upper deck only. They were joined by eleven more in June 1990, these also being allocated to Stockwell. This time they were put to use on the 196 (Norwood Junction–Brixton). They followed on as VC28 to VC38 (G128-38PGK). Another solitary example, VC39 (J139DGF) arrived in December 1991.

A number of the VC-class gained cherished registration marks between 1990 and 1994. VC23 was the first, gaining registration mark 23CLT in November 1990. In December, VC1, VC3 and VC25 became 101CLT, WLT803 and 125CLT. VC18 (G118NGN) followed in January 1991, becoming WLT818. Two more, VC6 and VC27, were re-registered to VLT60 and WLT837 in February. VC36 became 836DYE in July. The final VC to be re-registered in 1991 was VC11, becoming WLT311 in December. The first re-registration

C1 (C101CUL) was acquired by London Buses Limited to be trialled alongside V1 and V2 mentioned in the first chapter of this book. It is seen blinded for its journey on the 102 to Chingford Station. *Phil Hambling*

London Buses purchased thirty-nine Northern Counties bodied Volvo B10M Citybus double-deckers for use on the 133 and 196 from Stockwell. VC34 (G134PGK) is seen having a day out on the 189. *Ian Armstrong Collection*

in 1992 took place in May when VC29 (G129PGK) became 229CLT. It was followed in July by VC4, 14 and 39, these taking up new registration marks WLT474, 614DYE and 839DYE. VC19 and VC21 became 619DYE and 621DYE in May 1993. VC20 and VC28 became WLT920 and 528CLT in August 1993. VC12 was the last of the type to be re-registered. It was given the new identity of 585CLT in February 1994.

All thirty-nine passed to the newly privatised London General that November for continued use, with further information on their history being found under that heading later in this chapter.

LONDON & COUNTRY/KENTISH BUS/ARRIVA LONDON

London & Country had entered the LRT route tendering business in 1986 using a fleet of acquired Leyland Atlanteans. Approaching the renewal of these contracts, the company knew that they had to invest in new vehicles if they were to retain them and gain any new contracts. By 1989 the company had purchased a fleet of East Lancs bodied Dennis Dominators, trialling a Volvo Citybus demonstrator registered E825OMS at the same time. The trial seemed successful, with follow up orders being placed.

The first thirteen, 610-22 (G610-22BPH), arrived in September 1989 when they entered service from Addlestone garage. These East Lancs bodied double-deckers were initially used on the 110 (Twickenham–Hounslow/Cranford) and 131 (Weybridge/West Molesey–Wimbledon Station/Clapham Common). Both of these routes were lost upon re-tender in 1990, the Citybuses finding a new home on the 85 between Putney Bridge and Kingston. 614 was initially allocated to Reigate where it was used on the 727, joining the others at Addlestone later. They were used by the company, and the various incarnations, until May 1999 when they passed to Arriva Guildford & West Surrey. 611 (G611BPH) was retained at Beddington Farm, operating under the Arriva Croydon & North Surrey operation, passing to Arriva London South in October 1999, becoming L611 in that fleet. It was used by the latter company on the 403 alongside East Lancs bodied Leyland Olympians.

Twenty-five Northern Counties bodied B10M Citybus double-deckers were purchased at the same time as the East Lancs examples mentioned above. They followed on as 623 to 647 (G623-47BPH), also entering service in September 1989. They were split between Chelsham (625/33-8) and Dorking (623/4/6-31), with 639-43 being allocated directly to Godstone. Those at Chelsham were used on the 127 (Tooting Broadway–Purley), with the Dorking allocation finding work on the 293/393 (Epsom/Hackbridge–Morden Station/Merton Abbey Savacentre). However, allocation to these garages were short lived as both were sold off. Those at Chelsham were re-allocated to Godstone in October 1989, whilst the Dorking allocation moved to Leatherhead in March 1990. Godstone was subsequently closed in July 1990, meaning that they moved again, this time to the new garage at Beddington Farm, Croydon. These were then operated under the Londonlinks operation from January 1995, the latter operation being an amalgamation of London & Country and Kentish Bus's London operations. 632-8 moved again in August 1990, this time passing to the Kentish Bus garage at Dunton Green. This became an outstation of London & Country from where they operated the 320 between Bromley North and Biggin Hill Valley/Westerham. The final four, 644 to 647, were allocated to Crawley for use on local services and Green Line route 773.

631-9/41-3 transferred from Londonlinks to Kentish Bus in April 1996 along with route 320, retaining their former London & Country fleet numbers. The 320 went to Stagecoach Selkent a year later, with these buses moving to Dartford for use on the 96 (Dartford–Woolwich). The tender for the 96 was lost in the first part of 1999, with the Northern Counties bodied Citybuses moving to Arriva Medway Towns at Gillingham.

The latter part of 1990 saw London & Country penetrate deeper into Central London when they took over the operation of routes 78 (Shoreditch–Forest Hill) and 176 (Oxford Circus–Penge) in November, these being operated from a new temporary base at the Bricklayers Arms before a more permanent one was established at Newington Butts. To operate the routes, thirty-six East Lancs bodied Volvo B10M Citybus double-deckers were taken into stock. These followed on from the 1989 deliveries, becoming 648 to 665 and 667 to 684, these being registered H648-65/7-84GPF. Delivery took place between November 1990 and March 1991. 648-50/2-4/7/8 arrived in November, followed by 651/6, 667/9, 674-8 and 682/4 in December. 679, 681 and 683 entered the fleet in January 1991, with 662, 665, 670/2/3 arriving in February. 655/9/60/4/8 and 671 made up the numbers when they arrived in March. The delay in the delivery of these buses meant that the routes were covered by a mix of Leyland Atlanteans and Leyland Fleetlines that had been hired from Sheffield. The routes were re-allocated to the former London Transport Walworth garage in December 1992. The 78 was curtailed in March 1994 to terminate at Peckham Rye. In January 1995 Walworth was encompassed under the Londonlinks operation, meaning that these buses saw use on the 188 between Euston and Greenwich, working alongside Londonlinks Leyland Titans.

The 176 transferred to South London in July 1997, operating from Norwood, with route 188 following in August. The vehicles moved with the route, taking up new rolling stock numbers VE648 etc. and they transferred to Arriva London South in April 1998. These buses were withdrawn over the course of the year as they were cascaded out of London to Arriva Derby, Arriva Manchester, Arriva Midlands North, and Arriva Scotland West.

Ten single-door East Lancs bodied Citybuses were acquired from North Western in 1996. Four of these were allocated to the Londonlinks operation at Walworth from where they were used on the P3 (London Bridge–New Cross Garage). Arriving in July 1996 they took up stock numbers 701/4/5/10 (G640CHF, G643/7EKA, G661DTJ). The others found a home with Kentish Bus at Dartford, filling in the gaps as 702/3/6/7/8/9 (G641/2CHF, G648/9EKA, G659/60DTJ), these being taken into stock in October 1996. Their use on the P3 was short lived, the route passing to Stagecoach Selkent in November 1996. At this time, the four allocated to the route moved to Beddington Farm. In May 1998 the quartet was renumbered to 640, 643, 647 and 661 to avoid a clash of numbers at Beddington Farm.

In September 1989 thirteen East Lancs bodied Citybus double-deckers entered the London & Country fleet for use on the 110 and 131. 615 (G615BPH) is photographed on layover at Putney Bridge Station whilst operating the 85. *Ian Armstrong Collection*

A larger batch of twenty-five Northern Counties bodied Citybuses arrived later in 1989. 641 (G641BPH) is seen paused at Wallington Station on its way to Tooting Broadway whilst operating route 127. *Ian Armstrong Collection*

The largest fleet of Volvo B10M Citybus double-deckers arrived in 1990 for routes 78 and 176. East Lancs bodied Citybus 677 (H677GPF) was also later operated by Londonlinks, and is seen on the 188 to Euston. *Ian Armstrong Collection*

GREY GREEN

Grey Green purchased a pair of Volvo B10M-50 Citybus double-deckers with Alexander RV bodywork in November 1987. These coach-seated buses were used by the company on the Medway to London commuter services. These buses were numbered 104 and 105 (E104/5JYV) by the company.

Grey Green were successful in winning the contract for LRT route 24 (Hampstead Heath–Pimlico), taking the company through the heart of London, serving iconic locations such as Trafalgar Square, Whitehall and the Houses of Parliament. For the route, thirty

Alexander RV bodied Volvo Citybuses were purchased by the company, all of which wore the operator's distinctive grey, green and orange livery. Arriving earlier than needed, this fleet of buses initially saw service on routes 125 (North Finchley–Winchmore Hill) and 298 (Turnpike Lane–Cranbourne Road Industrial Estate/Clare Hall Hospital). Fleet numbers 115 to 144 were allocated to these buses, which carried registration marks F115-144PHM, the fleet being garaged at Grey Green's Stamford Hill coach garage. Little of interest happened during the operation of these buses on the route.

Grey Green was encompassed under the Arriva London group in January 1998, becoming Arriva London North East. Initially there was little change other than Arriva fleet names being placed on the Grey Green livery. However, they were slowly repainted into the Arriva 'cow horn' livery of red and white, being reclassed as 'VA' by Arriva. The type saw Sunday operation on route 19 (Finsbury Park–Battersea Bridge South Side) from February 1998, this continuing until March 2000. The buses along with route 24 were re-allocated to the former London Buses garage at Stamford Hill in March 1998. The 24 transferred from Stamford Hill to Tottenham in March 2000, with a number of the VAs moving with the route. VA115/6/8/9, 123-5 transferred to Wood Green in the July. Some of these allocations were short-lived, with some moving back to Arriva London North East at Barking.

115-144 were joined on the 24 in February 1990 by four additional dual-doored Citybuses. These followed on as 145 to 148 (G145-8TYT). As with those mentioned above, little of interest happened to the quartet whilst operating with Grey Green, and later Arriva London North East. All four were transferred to Tottenham garage in July 2000.

Six single-door Citybuses also arrived in February 1990. 149 to 154 (G149-54TYT) were taken into stock to update the rolling stock used on the 173 (North Finchley–Enfield), a route operated by Grey Green since October 1987. Allocated to Dagenham, these buses also saw service on the 275 (Walthamstow Central–Barkingside). They continued operating the 173 until October 1996, at which time the route passed to Capital Citybus. They were retained by Grey Green, and later Arriva London North East, until 1999, at which time they left London and were put to further use with Arriva Scotland West.

Four dual-door Citybuses, 155-8 (H155-8XYU), arrived in September 1990. They were initially ordered for use on the 168 between Hampstead Heath and Waterloo. However, allocated to Stamford Hill, they could be found on route 24, remaining true to this latter service until it was lost to Metroline in 2002. After this time they saw further use on Stamford Hill's garage routes until they left the fleet in the spring of 2003.

The company won a couple of LRT tenders from Thamesway in 1991, as they needed more double-deckers. At this time 104 and 105 were altered for standard bus work.

Grey Green were also successful in winning the tender for route 141 (Wood Green–Moorgate) in 1991, taking the route over from 1 February 1992. Rather than ordering new rolling stock, Grey Green rebodied sixteen of their Volvo B10M-61 coaches, nine of which were rebuilt as double-deckers. The other seven were rebuilt as single-deckers, which will feature later in this book. The nine double-deckers carried new East Lancs bodywork and were numbered 163-8, 170-2 by the company. These were registered B863-8/70-2XYR. Entering service on the 141 they remained on this route until June 1998. Under the ownership of Arriva London North East, they moved across to the 188 (Euston–North Greenwich). They were repainted into the standard red with white cow horns livery. They were replaced at Barking in 2003 by former Kentish Bus Leyland Olympians, after which time they were withdrawn. B864/70-2XYR saw further service in London when they were purchased by F E Thorpe of Wembley in March 2003; these being used on the 187 (Central Middlesex Hospital–Finchley Road O2 Centre) and 487 (South Harrow–Willesden Junction) with them. They were taken over by Metroline in August 2004 when Thorpes was acquired by them.

The Alexander bodied examples were sold in early 2003 via Fleetlink. Like the rebuilds mentioned above, they were replaced at Barking by ex-Kentish Bus Olympians. Four were acquired by Thorpes of Wembley, mainly for use on school contracts, but also routes 187 and 487. After these routes were lost on retender, they continued on rail replacement work. Metroline took over the Thorpe business in August 2004, including the four Volvos. They used them sporadically until January 2005, then stored them prior to sales to Ensign Bus.

115-8/23/5-7 were repainted in November 1996 in an all-over red livery for use on a rail replacement service for the Bakerloo Line between Oxford Circus and Elephant & Castle, these being given black fleet numbers at this time.

Grey Green introduced a splash of colour to Central London when they took on the 24 in 1989. 134 (F134PHM) shows this off as it heads towards Pimlico. *Ian Armstrong Collection*

Queen Elizabeth II celebrated her Golden Jubilee in 2002. Fifty London buses were decorated gold to join in with the celebrations. Arriva London's 157 (H157XYU) was one of the vehicles chosen. Gold vinyl was applied and retained by 157 until the end of the year.

The intake of low-floor buses in 2002 was the beginning of the end for the Citybuses with Arriva London. Those at Tottenham would see operation on the 73. The final VAs left Wood Green in December 2002. The type finally bowed out during 2003 when they were sold to Fleetlink of Liverpool. 115 (F115PHM) was repainted into Grey Green livery before being donated to the London Transport Museum in June 2003.

158 (H158XYU) was one of four Citybuses taken into stock in September 1990 for the 168. It is photographed on its way to Liverpool Street whilst on the 141. *Ian Armstrong Collection*

Members of the coaching fleet operating with Grey Green were converted to buses, some to double-deckers. This was the case with B870XYR, new as a coach, taking stock number 170 after conversion. *Ian Armstrong Collection*

(H157XYU) was one of fifty London buses that were decorated gold in 2002 to celebrate the late Queen Elizabeth II Golden Jubilee. It is seen heading north on the 24 to Hampstead Heath. *Ian Armstrong Collection*

BORO'LINE

Boro'line took on route 188 (Euston–Greenwich) in November 1989. They ordered fourteen Alexander bodied Volvo Citybuses for the route, but these were late in arriving. Until they were delivered, the route was operated by a mixture of Fleetlines and Atlanteans. It wasn't until March 1990 that the new rolling stock arrived wearing the blue, yellow, grey and red livery. Fleet numbers 921 to 934 were allotted to the batch which carried registration marks F101-14TML. Shortly after delivery it was found that the chassis and registration marks of five of the Citybuses did not tally up so they had to be altered. 926 F106TML became 929 F109TML; 927 F107TML became 926 F106TML; 929 F109TML was altered to 930 F110TML. 930 F110TML was changed to 931 F111TML, with 931 F111TML becoming 927 F107TML. They were operated from Crayford until the company

Although carrying route branded for the 188, Boro'lines's 927 (F107TML) is seen on layover in Bexleyheath whilst operating the 422. *Ian Armstrong Collection*

was taken over by Kentish Bus in February 1992. At this time the fourteen were renumbered 721 to 734 by their new owners, with them continuing to operate the 188. When Kentish Bus took over, the buses were moved to Dartford, the livery being altered to the maroon and primrose livery worn by Kentish Bus vehicles.

They later moved across to Cambridge Heath and these buses were put to use on the 78 (Shoreditch–Peckham Rye). In January 1998 the Cambridge Heath garage of Kentish Bus transferred to Arriva London North, the Citybuses transferring with them, gaining fleet numbers VA721/3-30/2/3. The 78 was moved to Stamford Hill at this time. The latter garage closed in March 2000; the remaining VAs being transferred to Tottenham. They did not last much longer, being withdrawn in the first half of 2000.

LONDON GENERAL

In November 1994 VC1-39 transferred to the new London General operation, owned by its management. The buses were repainted red, with a darker grey skirt and yellow lines. Under the new operator, many remained at Stockwell until withdrawal. VC16 got into trouble on 28 December 1994 when it was de-roofed under a low bridge at Norwood Junction. It was repaired and put back to use from Stockwell.

The coach seated VCs were transferred across to Sutton. One of these, VC3, was lent to sister company London Central in July and August 1998, used on the company's Coastal Clipper services. VC3 officially transferred to London Central in October, being allocated to New Cross, when VC1 was transferred to Merton.

The first of the VCs (VC11) were re-registered in October 1998. Registration mark WLT311 was altered for new G647SGT. VC1 (101CLT) was the second to be re-registered, to G101NGN, in May 1999. The first withdrawals took place in June 2001 when VC7-9 were sold. At this time VC1-6 moved to the private hire fleet; VC3-5 were transferred to London Central's New Cross garage, whilst VC1/2/6 were allocated to Sutton. VC10-39 were retained at Stockwell for the 133.

VC23 (23CLT) was re-registered to G123NGN in September 2001. The final VCs to be re-registered were VC4 (WLT474), VC6 (VLT60) and VC39 (839DYE), these becoming G867WGW, G886WGW and J227HMY, these all being done in August 2002. By October, the VC-class had been withdrawn.

LEYLAND LYNX

LONDON BUSLINES

Six Leyland Lynx saloons were purchased by London Buslines in 1987. These single-doored buses wore a livery of yellow with a chocolate skirt. Measuring 11.8m in length these buses were used on routes 81 (Hounslow–Slough) and 195 (Charville Lane Estate–Ealing Hospital), as well as a couple of routes in the Watford area on Sundays. These single-deckers carried registration marks D751-6DLO, taking fleet numbers 751-6. The first three arrived in May, with 754 following in June and 755/6 in July. London Buslines was acquired by Bee Line in October 1995, the Lynxes seeing further service in the Slough area. Less than a year later, in March 1996, the company was taken over by Centrewest, later becoming part of the First Group empire. The Lynxes saw further service with other First Group companies.

D752DLO was one of six Leyland Lynxes operated by London Buslines on routes 81 and 195. It is seen heading towards Slough on the 81. *Ian Armstrong Collection*

BORO'LINE/KENTISH BUS

In May 1987 three Leyland Lynxes were taken into stock by Boro'line. Numbered 227 to 229 these buses were registered D155-7HML. Initially used on Kent County Council contracts 22 (Bromley–Tunbridge Wells) and 26 (Sevenoaks–Kemsing loop), the Lynxes saw service on London routes 132 (Eltham Station–Bexleyheath), 422 (Bexleyheath Shopping Centre–Woolwich High Street) and 492 (Sidcup Station–Dartford) once they had been taken over by the company in 1988.

Twelve Leyland Lynxes were acquired by Boro'line in September and October 1989 for use on the 108 (Wanstead–Lewisham). Numbered 801 to 812 they were registered G34-45VME. 801-6 arrived in September, whilst 807-12 entered service in October.

Four more Lynxes arrived in January 1991 registered H813-6EKJ, taking up fleet numbers 813-6. These were used to replace ageing Leyland Nationals on the 492.

By the end of 1991 Boro'line were suffering from financial problems and in April 1992 the London area services were acquired by Kentish Bus, along with its vehicles. The original trio of Lynxes were re-allocated within Kentish Bus to Dunton Green. The other sixteen Lynxes remained operating the 108 and 492, these being reallocated from the former Boro'line Crayford premises to Dartford. Those used on the 108 were later moved to a base at Lewisham.

The loss of the 108 saw the Lynxes put to further use on a rail replacement contract for the North London Line. The route operated between Stratford and North Woolwich, the Lynxes working alongside Leyland Atlanteans. A blue, white and grey livery was worn by the buses which took up service on the route in May 1994. Ten Lynxes were allocated to Cambridge Heath.

The Lynxes that were not used on the North London Line contract were put to use on other services from both Dartford and Dunton Green, the others joining them at the end of 1995 when the North London Line contract finished. New route 233 (Eltham–Swanley)

Twelve Leyland Lynx saloons arrived with Boro'line in the autumn of 1989. G41VME was one of these vehicles which later passed to Kentish Bus. It is seen with this latter operator operating route 492 to Sidcup Station. *Ian Armstrong Collection*

saw Lynx operation from September 1996, also working alongside Leyland National Greenways on the 227 (Crystal Palace–Bromley).

The summer of 1999 saw many of the Lynxes depart Kentish Bus, either for Arriva Cymru or Arriva Kent & Sussex.

LONDON BUSES LIMITED

Eleven Leyland Lynxes were operated by London Buses Limited. They took stock of a demonstrator registered D573LDS, this being sourced from AA Services of Troon in February 1987. It was allocated to Peckham for the duration of its stay, being used on the 70 (Peckham–Victoria) before returning north during the same month.

The first two arrived with London Buses in December 1988, being allocated to Uxbridge where they were used on route 128. These had been purchased by the London Borough of Hillingdon and allocated to London Buses for use on the service which linked Uxbridge and Ruislip stations with Harefield and Mount Vernon Hospitals, these being located on the edge of the London Buses operating area. LX1 and LX2 (F101/2GRM) were painted into a special red and yellow livery similar to that worn by their predecessors, the Bristol LH BL-class and Leyland Nationals, the Lynxes working alongside the latter.

In August 1989 six Leyland Lynxes were taken into stock at Shepherds Bush garage. They were used to oust Leyland Nationals from route 283 (East Acton–Hammersmith). These followed on as LX3 to LX8 and were registered G73-8UYV. They wore the standard red livery complete with a yellow door. In January 1990 these buses transferred to Stamford Brook garage.

LX3-8 moved garages again in January 1994, this time being allocated to Hounslow where they saw service on the 81 between Hounslow and Slough. In November of the same year they passed to the privatised London United operation, gaining a repaint into the red, grey and white livery. They remained operating with London United until August 2000 when they were withdrawn from service. All six were sold to Kent-based operator Poynters of Wye.

A demonstrator registered F74DCW was loaned in December 1989 at Stamford Hill. However, it was not used in service and swiftly departed the fleet.

The final three Lynxes entered the London Buses Limited fleet in the same month. LX9 to LX11 arrived from Merthyr Tydfill at this time, joining LX1 and LX2 at Uxbridge. Like the latter two vehicles, these buses were owned by the London Borough of Hillingdon. They received the yellow and red livery used by buses operating the 128 and 129. Registered D105/6/11NDW they replaced the aging fleet of Leyland Nationals being used on the 128 and 129.

Above: **F102GRM was** new to London Buses Limited as LX2, being allocated to Uxbridge for use on the 128. It was later used on the 607 express service between Shepherds Bush and Uxbridge. It is this service that it is seen operating, carrying route branding for the service. *Ian Armstrong Collection*

Below: **Allocated to** Stamford Brook garage, LX4 (G74UYV) was taken into stock for use on the 283. However, it is seen operating a journey on the H23 to Stanwell Moor. *Ian Armstrong Collection*

LX10 and LX11 gained new registration marks 810DYE and 811DYE respectively in March 1990.

LX1/2/9-11 were sold to London Buses Limited in September 1991 at which time they received standard red livery. After this date route branding was applied for route 607 (Uxbridge–Shepherds Bush). The quintet remained operating the 607 through privatisation to Centrewest in September 1994.

COUNTY BUS

Eight new Leyland Lynxes were ordered by County Bus for delivery in 1990. H251-8GEV were numbered LX251-8 when they arrived in July. Allocated to Debden, an outstation of Harlow, they were used on route 66 which linked Romford Station and Leytonstone. Entering service in August 1990, they remained on the route until January 2001, transferring to the control of Arriva East Herts & Essex in 1998. At this time 251-3/6/7 moved to nearby Arriva Colchester, whilst 254/5/8 transferred across to the main Arriva the Shires fleet.

County Bus of Harlow took on LRT route 66 in August 1990 using eight Leyland Lynxes on the route. The last member of the batch, H258GEV, is photographed blinded for its return journey to Leytonstone. *Ian Armstrong Collection*

GREY GREEN

Grey Green used a small number of Leyland Lynxes for its London operations. Six arrived in October 1987 to work on the newly won 179 (Barking–Chingford). Registered E885-90KYW they arrived wearing a white-based livery, relieved by orange skirts and a chocolate cantrail. Stock numbers 885 to 890 were allocated to these buses. After the assumption of route 24 in 1988 a new livery was introduced of grey, green and orange, the Lynxes soon receiving this livery. They also saw service on the 313 (Potters Bar Station–Chingford Station) and the 379 (Chingford Station–Yardley Lane Estate).

Like London Buses, Grey Green took stock of three former Merthyr Tydfill Lynxes, arriving in November 1989. Taking up stock numbers 801 to 803 they carried registration marks D101/2/8NDW.

In September 1990 the Lynxes were put to use on the 210, standing in for the late-running of the intended rolling stock, with double-deckers in turn replacing the Lynxes on the 179.

Grey Green retained the Lynxes until 1996, with 888 and 889 moving on to Arriva East Herts & Essex; the others being used further by Arriva Maidstone & District.

ATLAS BUS

Route 112 (Ealing Broadway–Wood Green) passed to Pan Atlas in July 1988. Eight new Leyland Lynxes were taken into stock by the company to operate the route. They wore a white livery relieved by a grey skirt and red and blue diagonal stripes. Registered E299, 328OMG and E965-70PME they were numbered AB51/5/7/2/3/6/4/8. A second route, the 107 (Edgware–New Barnet), was won by Pan Atlas in October 1991. Although the latter route was operated by Olympians, these and the Lynxes could often be found on both services. They were renumbered in July 1994 using the last two digits of their registration marks, with the class code 'LL'. The 112 was lost in August 1994, passing to R&I Coaches. The Lynxes were sold by the end of the year.

METROBUS

A Leyland Lynx demonstrator registered D634BBV was lent to Metrobus for a couple of days in July 1987. Just over a year later, in September 1988, a solitary Lynx arrived with the company registered F80SMC. It was used from Green Street Green on route 361 (Bromley North–Green Street Green). It also saw service on the 354 between Bromley North and Croydon.

Metrobus was a third operator in the Greater London area to acquire some of the former Merthyr Tydfill Leyland Lynxes. D103/4/10NDW arrived with the company in December 1989. They were used to replace the Bedford saloons operating on the 354, also being used on the 356 (Croydon–Biggin Hill/Sevenoaks).

Another two second-hand Lynxes were taken into stock in March 1991 from Miller of Foxton, Cambridgeshire. These carried registration marks F165/6SMT. They settled with the company, joining the other Leyland Lynxes in the fleet on routes 353, 354, 356 and 357. They were also found on route 261 (Lewisham–Green Street Green) at weekends.

The final Lynx to be purchased by Metrobus was acquired from Volvo Training School, and was the only example of the Lynx II model to be operated. Registered K101JMV it was taken into stock during August 1992.

The two former Miller Bus Lynxes were first to leave the fleet, doing so in May 2002 and March 2003 respectively along with the former Merthyr Lynxes. F80SMC was sold to Ensign Bus in December 2004. K101JMV was the last to leave, departing the Metrobus fleet for Ensign in July 2006. In 2013 it entered preservation.

LONDON & COUNTRY/LONDONLINKS

Six Leyland Lynxes were purchased by London & Country in December 1989 for use on their LRT tendered route 289 (Elmers End–Croydon Airport). Wearing the two-tone green livery they were numbered 311 to 316 (G311-6DPA). Originally allocated to Godstone, they moved to the newly opened Beddington Farm garage in August 1990. In January 1995 the six came under the control of the newly formed Londonlinks, only to return to London & Country ownership in January 1998. Shortly after, they came under control of Arriva Croydon & North Surrey. These Lynxes did not operate long for their new owner, departing for Arriva Cymru in August 1998.

Two more, D101/2NDW, were acquired from Maidstone & District in August 1996. These had previously operated with Grey Green and were numbered 399 and 400 in the Londonlinks fleet. The pair were pressed into service on the 289 with the other six, being repainted into the two-tone green livery. These were withdrawn in September 1998, passing to Arriva Kent & Sussex.

CENTREWEST/FIRST LONDON

As mentioned above, LX1/2/9-11 were privatised to Centrewest on 2 September 1994. November 1995 saw LX2 (F102GRM) reregistered 292CLT. Further re-registrations took place in February 1998 when LX10 and LX11 lost their cherished marks 810/811DYE in favour of D875/6ELL. Their careers in London came to an end under the First Group days, with LX1/2/9 passing to neighbouring First Beeline in 1997, whilst others left the following year.

First Centrewest acquired two additional Leyland Lynxes for use on school routes. The first, 62666 (J916WVC), arrived from First Devon & Cornwall in September 2004. Wearing First livery, the bus was in a bad state and underwent repair at First Berkshire's Bracknell garage before entering service on school route 646 in March 2005. It remained with the company until withdrawal in September 2008. The second was registered H859GRE. Numbered 60093 it was sourced from First Somerset & Avon in October 2004. It lasted less than a year, being sold for scrap in 2005.

***Above*: A pair** of Leyland Lynxes were acquired by Metrobus from Cambridgeshire independent operator Millers of Foxton. The first of these, F165SMT, is seen in full Metrobus livery blinded for route 354 to Bromley North. *Ian Armstrong Collection*

***Below*: 1988 saw** Pan Atlas take over service 112, purchasing eight Leyland Lynxes for use on the route. E299OMG was one of these and is seen attending the North Weald bus rally. *Ian Armstrong Collection*

RENAULT PR100

Just two examples of the Renault PR100 saloon were used in London. A Northern Counties bodied example was used by London Buses Limited from Seven Kings garage in March and April 1989. It saw service on the 150 (Ilford Station–Chigwell Row).

A second PR100, also bodied by Northern Counties, arrived at Seven Kings in November 1989 for evaluation against the Optare Delta and Scania L113CRL saloons. Registered G276VML, this bus was allocated fleet number RN1. Loaned from Renault Vehicles, Dunstable it was also used on the 150. It remained operational with East London until 1993 when it left the Capital for further use with Scunthorpe-based Hornsby, where it worked alongside F100AKB.

RN1 (G276VML) was one of two Renault PR100 single-deckers to be taken into stock by London Buses Limited. Although predominantly used on the 150, it is photographed on its way to Romford Market on the 129. *Ian Armstrong Collection*

DENNIS FALCON

London & Country was the only operator to use the Dennis Falcon on a LRT-tendered route. Ten 48-seaters were purchased in March 1990 and took up fleet numbers 301 to 310 (G301-10DPA). Allocated to Godstone, the first five of these were used on the 289 (Elmers End–West Croydon), working alongside Leyland Lynxes. They were also used on route 414 to Reigate. The type was short-lived, with 301/6-10 moving to the Midlands for further use, with others being transferred within London & Country itself.

Ten Dennis Falcons were used by London & Country on the 289. 304 (G304DPA) represents these single deckers and is seen loading at West Croydon bus station on its way to Purley. *Ian Armstrong Collection*

VOLVO B10M/B10B

Introduced in 1978 the Volvo B10 chassis range remained in production until 2001, at which time it was replaced by low-floor models. The B10M was the most popular chassis in the range, this mainly being built as a coach. The B10M was also found underneath single-deckers, with a handful of these operating in the Greater London area.

GREY GREEN

Grey Green took on the contract for the 210 (Finsbury Park–Brent Cross Shopping Centre) in September 1990. Thirteen Volvo B10M-55s were ordered for the service, these being bodied by East Lancs

Thirteen East Lancs bodied Volvo B10M saloons were purchased by Grey Green for use on the 210. 916 (H916XYT) is seen paused at Brent Cross Shopping Centre on its way to Finsbury Park Station. *Ian Armstrong Collection*

with the EL2000 model. They took up rolling stock numbers 912-923/5 (H912-23/5XYT). In May 1993 these buses were being used on the 125. The 210 was lost to F E Thorpe in 1998.

Route 179 was taken over by Grey Green in 1992. Rather than buying new rolling stock, the company rebodied seven of its Volvo B10M coaches with East Lancs EL2000 bodywork. These were numbered 855 to 861 (A855/6UYM, B857-61XYR). These operated the route for five years before being replaced by new low-floor Dennis Dart SLF saloons. After this, these buses transferred to sister company County Bus, Harlow, moving on to Arriva Colchester in the summer of 1997.

Seven Grey Green Volvo B10M coaches were rebodied in 1992 when more rolling stock was needed following the takeover of route 179. 855 (A855UYM) was one of those converted and is seen above operating a journey on route 20 at Walthamstow. *Ian Armstrong Collection*

A fleet of Alexander PS bodied Volvo B10Ms were operated for a short period of time in the Romford area of north-east London. 412 (M412RRN) came on loan to Stagecoach East London from Stagecoach Ribble in April 1995. It is seen operating route 247 to Romford Station. *Ian Armstrong Collection*

STAGECOACH LONDON

Stagecoach London briefly operated a fleet of Volvo B10M single-deckers during 1995. 625 (L625TDY), an Alexander PS bodied example was lent to Stagecoach Selkent at Catford on 16 March 1995, arriving from Coastline Buses of Worthing.

A month later, in April, ten similar buses were lent to Stagecoach East London. 401-4 (L341-4KCK, 409/10 (L339/40KCK) and 411-4 (M411-4RRN) were loaned from Ribble Motor Services. They were used to replace the fleet of Volvo B6 saloons used in the Barking and

Romford areas. They moved on to East Midlands Motor Services in July.

Three more, 662-4 (M662-4ECD), were loaned from Hampshire Bus in May and June 1995, these operating from Romford on the 247 until August. 663 was used as a driver training vehicle. The trio, as well as the 10 Alexander PS saloons, operated in the Stagecoach stripe livery.

CAPITAL CITYBUS

Capital Citybus operated a pair of Duple Dominant bodied Volvo B10M saloons. Registered D497/9MYS were given fleet numbers 797 and 799 when they arrived at Dagenham in September 1996. They were acquired from Eastbourne Buses to cover an increase on school route 646.

AEC REGENT V

London Buses Limited purchased a former East Kent Park Royal bodied AEC Regent V from Wealden PSV in May 1991. It was allocated to the Leaside Buses division at Stamford Hill. Registered GJG750D it was allocated rolling stock number RV1. This manual gearbox double-decker was used as a driver training vehicle by Leaside, as well as a private hire bus.

It was privatised to the Leaside Buses operation in September 1994, remaining with them until the 27 October 1997. On this date

RV1 (GJG750D) was a more unusual purchase by London Buses Limited. It was placed into the Leaside Travel fleet, being used as both a private hire and driver training vehicle. *Liam Farrer-Beddall*

the Leaside Travel operation, based at Edmonton garage at this time, was transferred to the control of County Bus & Coach, and later Arriva East Herts & Essex. A re-organisation of Arriva's operations in London and the Home Counties saw the Edmonton garage and the Leaside Travel operation transfer back to the control of Arriva London North on 3 October 1998.

It remained with Arriva until December 2005, at which time it passed to Ensign Bus.

DENNIS LANCE

LONDON BUSES

The Dennis Lance was another type of single-decker purchased by London Buses Limited in an attempt to replace the ageing fleet of Leyland Nationals. Having purchased several types already mentioned in this book, Dennis Lance saloons were introduced in 1992.

The first sixteen arrived in the first half of 1992, being numbered LA1 to LA16 by the company, these carrying registration marks J101-10, 411, 112-6WSC. LA1 and LA5 arrived in April, whilst LA2-4/6-15 in May, with LA16 arriving in June. They were allocated to Selkent's Catford garage, wearing a red, white and black livery, complete with a grey skirt. They were put to use on the 36B (Grove Park–Camberwell Green–Victoria), replacing Routemasters on the service. Despite being 11.7m in length, these saloons seated only thirty-nine.

A pair of Dennis Lance demonstrators were taken on loan by London Buses that summer. The first arrived at Catford in August 1992. Registered J215OCW this single-decker carried a Northern Counties Paladin body and wore Merseybus livery. The second was bodied by Alexander, arriving in September at Seven Kings garage wearing a green and white livery and was registered J110SPB.

The largest fleet of Dennis Lances entered service with London Buses in 1993, being allocated to Metroline. LN1 to LN10 (K301YJA etc) arrived in February and were allocated to Willesden for route 302 (Mill Hill Broadway–Notting Hill Gate). LN11 (K311YJA) arrived in April and was also allocated to Willesden. This single-decker was sent to Malaysia for a few months before returning to London in August 1993. LN11 was preceded by the delivery of LN12 to LN19 (K312-9YJA), all of which arrived in March. LN20-31 (K320-31YJA) completed delivery of these buses, arriving in April. LN12-31 were placed into store at North Wembley for a while before moving to their intended garage, Cricklewood. They entered service from Cricklewood in September on route 113 between Edgware and Oxford Circus.

The final step-entrance Dennis Lance saloons were taken into stock by Selkent in early 1994. The Plaxton Verde body style was chosen this time. Wearing a livery of red, white, black and grey these 11m long saloons were allocated to Catford where they were used on the 208 (Lewisham–Orpington). LV1/3-6 (L201YAG etc) were first to arrive in February, followed by LV2/7-11 (L202YAG etc) in March. LV12 (L212YAG) was the final member of the twelve to arrive, doing so in April, being re-registered the same month to WLT461.

LA1-16 and LV1-12 passed to Stagecoach Selkent in September. LA1-16 were transferred to sister company Stagecoach East London in July 1995, these being allocated to Barking for the 145 (Leytonstone–Dagenham Asda). They lost their original livery in favour of all-red with white fleet names. LA1-16 were converted to single-door layout in 1997 before leaving London, transferring to Stagecoach Ribble. LV1-12 were transferred from the 208 to the 75 (West Croydon–Lewisham), but they were still used on the 208.

In October 1994, the LNs transferred to the newly privatised Metroline operation. The LNs were found to be too long for the 302, this resulting in the transfer of Willesden's allocation (LN1-11) to Cricklewood where they were used on the 32 (Edgware Station–Kilburn Park Station). Metroline started to repaint the LNs into the red with a blue skirt livery during 1995. The LNs were withdrawn from service in October 1997, being replaced by M-class MCW Metrobuses. They were placed into store for a number of years before finding new owners.

The LV-class Dennis Lances were transferred from Catford to Bromley in November 1997 where they were put to use on the 227 (Bromley North–Crystal Palace). They lasted on the 227 until March 2000 when they were replaced by low-floor Dennis Dart SLF saloons. Later in the year the LVs, with the exception of LV8, were transferred to Stagecoach South East.

CAPITAL CITYBUS

A solitary Alexander PS bodied Dennis Lance was purchased by Capital Citybus in September 1998. Registered M796MPM the saloon was new to Dennis, Guildford in 1995, being used by them as a demonstrator. Taking up rolling stock number 796, it was used on the single-deck routes in the Ilford area. It remained with Capital Citybus through First ownership. February 2005 saw the saloon renumbered DB67296. It was withdrawn in mid-2006, passing to First Western National in September 2006.

ARRIVA LONDON

London & Country purchased fifteen East Lancs EL2000 bodied Dennis Lance saloons for use in the Crawley area in February 1996, these being numbered LS10-24 (N210-21, 322, 223-4TPK). LS10-19 transferred to Arriva Croydon & North Surrey in July 1998. This latter operation transferred to the control of Arriva London South in October 1999, with LS10-9 passing to the new owner. Renumbered DL10 to DL19, they were used on the 289 between Elmers End, Croydon and Purley. They were soon repainted red and remained on the 289 for just over a year before being replaced by low-floor single-deckers. These eleven single-deckers transferred to Arriva Merseyside in January 2001.

Above: **Catford garage** took stock of sixteen Alexander bodied Dennis Lance single-deckers in 1992. Wearing a red, white and grey livery, these buses were used on route 36B. The second member of the batch, LA2 (J102WSC) is photographed passing through Lewisham on its way to Grove Park. *Ian Armstrong Collection*

Below: **The following** year saw twenty-nine Dennis Lance saloons taken into stock by London Buses Limited and allocated to Metroline. LN29 (K329YJA) is seen on its way to Willesden Bus Garage whilst on route 302. *Ian Armstrong Collection*

Above: **Route 113** was also the recipient of the Northern Counties bodied Dennis Lance saloons. LN24 (K324YJA) is seen travelling along Oxford Street shortly before completing its journey at Oxford Circus. *Ian Armstrong Collection*

Below: **1994 saw** the arrival of the last step-entrance Dennis Lance saloons in London. Twelve Plaxton Verde bodied examples arrived with Selkent, joining the LA-class Lances at Catford garage. LV7 (L207YAG) is seen heading towards Orpington on route 208 wearing its red, white and grey livery. *Ian Armstrong Collection*

VOLVO B10B, B10L, B10LA, B10BLE

LONDON BUSES

Thirteen Northern Counties Paladin bodied Volvo B10B saloons were purchased by London Buses Limited in early 1993. Allocated to the London General division, they were put to use on the 88 between Oxford Circus and Clapham Common. Rolling stock numbers VN1 to VN13 were allocated to the single-deckers, these carrying registration marks K100KLL, K2-13KLL. Added to the fleet based at Stockwell, these saloons were branded 'The Clapham Omnibus'. In November 1994 these thirteen single-deckers passed to the privatised London General company, remaining on the route until April 1997 when MCW Metrobuses replaced them. After this time they transferred to the Oxford Bus Company.

The fleet of Northern Counties bodied Volvo B10B saloons gained Clapham Omnibus fleet names. This can be seen in the view above of VN1 (K100KLL). *Ian Armstrong Collection.*

The final member of the thirteen VN-class Volvo B10Bs can be seen heading towards Oxford Circus on route 88. VN13 (K13KLL) is also seen carrying the Clapham Omnibus fleet names. *Ian Armstrong Collection*

LONDON SUBURBAN

London Suburban operated four Volvo B10B saloons, these being bodied by Northern Counties. They arrived from parent company Liverbus in July 1993, registered K101-4CHF. They took up fleet numbers 101 to 104 and were used on the 271 (Highgate Village–Finsbury Square/Liverpool Street Bus Station) alongside a fleet of Volvo Olympians. These passed to MTL London Northern in April 1995 for continued use on the 271.

STAGECOACH LONDON

No other orders for the B10B or B10L models were placed by London operators. Stagecoach Selkent took stock of two demonstrators during

1995. The first arrived at the end of April registered M967GDU. This Plaxton Verde bodied Volvo B10B saloon was used from Catford on the 208, operating in a white with blue stripe livery.

A couple of months later, in June, an Alexander Ultra bodied Volvo B10L saloon registered M394KRW was operated by Stagecoach East London from Upton Park garage. It was put to use on the 101 (North Woolwich–Wanstead), working alongside the fleet of SLW-class Scania L113CRL single-deckers.

LONDON UNITED

London United also took a Volvo B10B saloon on loan in 1995. This Wright bodied example was registered M310KHP and was used by the company on the 267 (Hammersmith–Fulwell Garage) from Fulwell garage for a week at the end of June, beginning of July 1995. Like M967GDU with Stagecoach, M310KHP was operated in non-red, wearing a silver-based livery with a grey skirt and blue stripe.

LEASIDE

Leaside was the only other operator to use a Volvo B10L saloon on an LRT contract. An Alexander Ultra bodied demonstrator registered L456JCK was used for a day on the 144 (Edmonton Green–Muswell Hill Broadway).

ARRIVA THE SHIRES

Arriva the Shires purchased a number of Volvo B10BLE saloons with Wright Crusader bodywork. Three of these (3258-60 V258-60HBH) were put to use on the H18 (Harrow–Harrow Weald–Northwick Park–Harrow), these arriving in November 1999. The route was won from Metroline. They arrived late so Dennis Dart saloons stood in for them until they arrived. The H18 was originally operated from High Wycombe, before moving to a more logical Garston garage in 2005. They were delivered in the turquoise and cream livery, being repainted red in 2006. The trio were replaced on the H18 in 2006,

November 2000 saw the arrival of three Wright Crusader bodied Volvo B10BLE saloons for use on the H18 in the Harrow area. The first of these, 3258 – V258HBH – is seen blinded for its journey to Harrow Weald. *Ian Armstrong Collection*

becoming regulars on the 288, 303 and 305. Their time on London routes came to an end in May 2010 when they were repainted and put to use on local services in the Watford area. 3260 was destroyed by fire in 2013, whilst 3258 went into storage at Stevenage and 3259 transfer to Harlow for further use.

TELLINGS-GOLDEN MILLER

Route 726 (Bromley–Heathrow Airport) was acquired by Tellings-Golden Miller in 1999 along with the business of Capital Logistics. A fleet of Ikarus bodied DAF SB200s were operating the route at the time of acquisition. To update the rolling stock on the route,

Tellings-Golden Miller ordered a fleet of seven Alexander ALX300 bodied Volvo B10BLE saloons. Arriving late in April 2000 carrying registration marks W901-7UJM, these saloons wore the white, yellow and blue livery. Originally operating from West Drayton, these seven buses later moved to Fulwell where they continued to operate the route. They remained on the service until April 2005 when the contract was lost to Metrobus. By this time the route had been renumbered X26 and altered to operate between West Croydon and Heathrow. After this, Tellings-Golden Miller had no use for them so they left London for other operators in the Status Group.

The fleet of single-deckers used on the 726 were upgraded in 2000. Seven Alexander ALX300 bodied Volvo B10BLE saloons arrived in April including W907UJM, seen travelling along Bath Road before reaching Heathrow Airport. *Ian Armstrong Collection*

FIRST LONDON

First London took four Wright Fusion bodied Volvo B10LA articulated buses on loan in the autumn of 2001. They were trialled on route 207 between Shepherds Bush and Hayes Bypass, working alongside a pair of Volvo B7LA buses. AV10 (V610GGB) was first to arrive, doing so in September, followed by AV6 to AV8 (V606-8GGB) in October. All four were sourced from First Glasgow. They were retained by First London until May 2002 when they left London, passing to First Bristol for further use.

AV7 (V607GGB) is photographed on its way to Shepherds Bush on route 207. AV7 was one of four of the type to be taken on loan by First London. *Ian Armstrong Collection*

DENNIS LANCE SLF

LONDON BUSES LIMITED

London Buses Limited were beginning to look at low-floor buses just prior to privatisation. Alongside the Scania L113CRL, thirty-eight 10.8m Wright Pathfinder 320 bodied Dennis Lance SLF saloons were purchased by the company and split between three of the operating divisions.

The first ten were allocated to London United, the first of which arriving at the end of 1993. They were allocated to Hounslow where they were used on the 120 between Hounslow Bus Station and Northolt Station, entering service at the end of January 1994. Fleet numbers LLW1 to LLW10 (ODZ8901-10) were the buses used on the route. LLW1/2/4/5 arrived in December 1993, with LLW3/6-10 following in January 1994.

The next fourteen were allocated to Centrewest for use in the Uxbridge area. Following on as LLW11-24 (ODZ8911-24), these were used on the 222 (Uxbridge Station–Hounslow Bus Station). LLW11 was first to arrive, doing so in December 1993. LLW12-5/7/9 were next to arrive in February 1994. Delivery of these single-deckers was complete in March 1994 when LLW16/8/20-4 put in an appearance. LLW17 went on loan to Badgerline in Bath between February and March 1994.

The outstanding fourteen were allocated to Metroline's Harrow Weald garage. LLW25 to LLW38 (L25-9, 21, 31/2/9/3-8WLH were used on the 186 between Brent Cross and Northwick Park Hospital. LLW25 was first to put in an appearance in January 1994. LLW26, 34/5/8 were next to arrive in April and LLW36 in May. Delivery was complete in June when LLW27-33/7 arrived with the company.

LLW11-24 were first to be privatised, when Centrewest was brought by its management in September 1994. Metroline's allocation were next to be privatised when the company was sold in October 1994. LLW1 to LLW10 were the last of the thirty-eight to be privatised. London United was sold by London Buses Limited in November 1994.

CENTREWEST/FIRST LONDON

LLW11-24 passed to Centrewest and remained on the 222 until the route was lost to London United in 2000. Centrewest also used the LLWs on the 27 (Camden Town–Turnham Green) and 92 (Ealing Hospital–St Raphael's Estate). A Wright Pathfinder bodied Dennis Lance SLF was lent in June to Centrewest from Badgerline. M138FAE was the vehicle concerned and joined the LLWs on the 222 at Uxbridge.

An additional Wright Pathfinder bodied Dennis Lance SLF was acquired by First Centrewest in September 1998. M221EAF was sourced from First Leeds and allotted rolling stock number LLW31, the fleet number clashing with a similar vehicle operating with Metroline. Again allocated to Uxbridge it was used on the 335 between Slough and Chalfont & Latimer Station.

Both the 27 and 92 were restocked with double-deck buses in early 2001. After this time the LLWs moved to First Southern National and First Bristol for further use. LLW31 was retained until the end of 2002, at which time it moved on to First Midland Red.

METROLINE

Metroline's contingent, LLW25-38, remained at Harrow Weald for use on the 186. They were later repainted into a red and blue livery, the two colours being separated by a white band. They remained operating from Harrow Weald on the 186 until September 2000. At this time the route, and the LLWs, were transferred to Edgware. They remained operating the 186 until withdrawal in 2006. After this time they were sold for further use around the UK, with three finding homes in Malta.

LONDON UNITED

Very little of interest happened with LLW1-10 under London United ownership. In March 2000 the ten saloons transferred to Hounslow Heath garage when the 120 was allocated a fleet of low-floor double-deckers. From their new home they were used on the H91 (Hounslow West–Hammersmith). At the time of transfer, Hounslow Heath was under the control of Westlink, the latter operation being subsumed by London United in September of the same year. They received the smart red, white and grey livery.

In June 2001 the LLWs moved again, this time to Stamford Brook, remaining on the H91, only to return to Hounslow Heath in May 2002. They were replaced by a fleet of low-floor Dennis Dart SLF saloons in July 2004. However, the LLWs were retained, being used on the Christmas park & ride service K50 at the end of 2004. This was to be their last route, passing to A2Z Buses of Birmingham.

The first ten Wright Pathfinder bodied Dennis Lance SLF saloons were allocated to London United for use on the 120. The first of these, LLW1 (ODZ8901) is seen heading towards Northolt Station. *Ian Armstrong Collection*

Above: **Centrewest were** allocated the second batch of Dennis Lance SLFs purchased by London Buses Limited. Uxbridge Station provides the backdrop for this photograph of LLW24 (ODZ8924) which is seen on its way to Hounslow. *Ian Armstrong Collection*

Below: **The third** and final batch of LLW-class bodied Dennis Lance SLFs were delivered to Metroline. LLW28 (L28WLH) is photographed at Brent Cross bus station before heading back to Northwick Park Hospital. *Ian Armstrong Collection*

COUNTY BUS

Four single-doored Dennis Lance SLFs were purchased by County Bus & Coach in November 1994, these again carrying Wright Pathfinder bodywork. Wearing a pale cream and dark green skirt livery, they were branded 'Townlink' and were put to use by the company on the 502 between Romford and Harlow. They were numbered ELW266 to ELW269 (M266-9VPU).

County Bus was acquired by the Cowie Group in February 1996, which in turn was re-branded as Arriva in 1998. Under Arriva ownership, County Bus was renamed Arriva East Herts & Essex, which was later combined with Arriva the Shires. ELW269 was taken off the 502 in February 1999 and moved to Arriva Southend, whilst the others remained at Harlow until September 2002, at which time they moved to Luton.

ELW269 (M269VPU) was the last of four Wright Pathfinder bodied Dennis Lance SLF saloons purchased by County Bus & Coach for use on the 502 (Romford–Harlow). Romford Station provides the backdrop to this photograph, with ELW269 showing off the route branding applied to these buses. *Mike Harris*

LONDON & COUNTRY

Four Wright Pathfinder 320 bodied Dennis Lance SLFs were purchased by London & Country in January 1995. Numbered 517 to 520 (M517-20KPA) they were allocated to Guildford (517-9) and Leatherhead (520) for use on the 408 (West Croydon–Guildford). These single-door buses wore a two-tone green livery, relieved by a red band. A fifth example arrived in December 1995 registered N527SPA, this taking up rolling stock number LSL9. The others were renumbered LSL5-8 in 1998. They were sent to Arriva North West in April 2001, with the exception of LSL8 which was retained by Arriva Guildford & West Surrey until June 2005, at which time it moved within Arriva Southern Counties, passing to Arriva Kent & Sussex at Tunbridge Wells.

London & Country also took stock of four Wright Pathfinder bodied Dennis Lance SLF saloons for use on a route into Greater London. 517 (M517KPA) was the first of the quartet used on the 408 and is seen loading at West Croydon bus station before returning to Guildford. Like County Bus & Coach, London & Country also applied route branding to their Lance SLFs. *Mike Harris*

MAN 11.190/ OPTARE VECTA

R&I, MTL LONDON, METROLINE

Five MAN 11.190 saloons were ordered by R&I Tours in 1995 for use on the 112 (Ealing Broadway–Brent Cross). Two arrived with the company in June 1995 registered M507/8ALP. Three more arrived in September carrying registration marks N701-3FLN, carrying Optare Vecta bodywork. These took up fleet numbers 249 to 253 with the company. R&I Tours was purchased in October 1995 by MTL Holdings, being placed under the control of London Northern. The silver and blue livery originally worn by these single-deckers gave way to an all-over red livery, with white flashes. They were renumbered MV249-53 by their new owners. MTL London Northern itself was acquired by Metroline in August 1998, the MAN 11.190 saloons passing to Metroline at this time. Another repaint was received by these buses, complete with a blue skirt. They were retained by Metroline until the summer of 2001, at which time they were put into store at North Wembley before being sold in September.

WESTLINK, LONDON UNITED

A pair of Optare Vecta bodied MAN 11.190 saloons were taken on loan by Westlink prior to the company taking a small fleet of their own. L822XMR was the first, used in an all-white livery relieved by grey, blue and yellow flashes. It was used for a week in mid-January 1995 on the 371. A second demonstrator, M957VWY, was lent to Westlink at Kingston during July 1995.

Eight similar single-deckers were delivered to Westlink in July and August 1995. Registered N281-8DWY, these buses were numbered

VA1 to VA8 upon arrival. They were allocated to Hounslow Heath for use on the 371 (Kingston–Richmond). They wore the red with turquoise and white stripes livery associated with the company. VA3 was stolen at the end of July 1995, causing damage to the vehicle which was soon repaired.

London United acquired Westlink in September 1995, the VAs included. However, London United were using the VA classification code for their fleet of Volvo Olympians. This meant that the MANs were renumbered MV1 to MV8.

From 1 August 1995 the 371 and the MVs were transferred from Hounslow Heath to Kingston. Route branding was applied to the eight singles in 1997, along with the London United livery. The Westlink name and licence was retained until September 2000, at which time Kingston garage was officially transferred to London

N702FLN was one of five Optare Vecta bodied MAN 11.190 single-deckers to be purchased by R&I Buses in 1995. Delivered in September, N702FLN passed to MTL London in October. It is seen loading at Golders Green bus station before heading towards Finchley Road. *Ian Armstrong Collection*

Westlink took eight Optare bodied MAN 11.190 saloons during the summer of 1995. The first of these, VA1 – N281DWY, is seen loading at Cromwell Road Bus Station, Kingston whilst operating the 371 to Richmond. *Ian Armstrong Collection*

United, at which time the MVs were transferred. The latter garage was closed in December 2001, being replaced by one at Tolworth, MV1-8 making the move to the new facility. However, their career on the 371 came to an end in January 2002 when they were replaced by Dennis Dart SLFs. They soon found use as driver training buses at both Stamford Brook and Tolworth, remaining with London United until 2012 or 2013.

VOLVO B6BLE

LONDON GENERAL

London General took stock of a solitary Volvo B6LE saloon complete with Wright Crusader bodywork on long-term loan in August 1995. It was used by the company from Merton on the 200 (Raynes Park–Streatham, Telford Avenue) and 201 (Tulse Hill–Mitcham). A restricted turn on the 200 at Atkinson Morley Hospital meant it was mostly used on the 201. However, it also saw service on the 155 (Wimbledon–Stockwell) and 355 (Mitcham–Elephant & Castle). Numbered VWL1 it was registered N101HGO, wearing the red with grey skirt livery. VWL1 was originally to have been registered M220EGF, but was re-registered N101HGO by Volvo before entering service. VWL1 transferred from Merton to Sutton in October 1998 and in the same year, VWL1 was put to use on a free Tesco shuttle service in Epsom.

It had left London by early 1999, returning to Volvo. It was later lent out by Duffields of Cambridge, seeing service with a number of operators, including Metropolitan Omnibus Company on the 187 in September 1999.

TRAVEL LONDON

Travel London won the contract for the C1 (Victoria–Kensington), starting on 13 June 1998. The company ordered a fleet of Optare Solos for the route which were late, not arriving until December 1998. Their place was taken by a fleet of Wright Crusader bodied Volvo B6LE saloons registered R582-7/9-91YON and R606YON. These were loaned from parent company Travel West Midlands and worked the route alongside Optare Excels until the end of the year.

LONDON TRAVELLER/METROPOLITAN OMNIBUS/ THORPES

Harlesden-based London Traveller gained the contracts for routes 187 (Queens Park–Central Middlesex Hospital) and 487 (Willesden Junction–South Harrow Station), taking them over in September 1999. A Wright bodied Volvo B6BLE demonstrator was taken into stock briefly for use on the two routes, this being registered T290ROF. Finance was provided by Yorkshire Traction to purchase new buses for the two routes. Fifteen low-floor East Lancs Spryte bodied Volvo B6BLEs were ordered for the routes. Registered V501-15EFR, these buses wore an all-red livery with a yellow band on the side. The first nine arrived in August, with V510-5EFR putting in an appearance during September. Five more arrived in April 2000 registered W516-9/21CCK.

The name of the company changed in September 2000, becoming the Metropolitan Omnibus. Following the change of name, the yellow

Routes 187 and 487 were taken over by London Traveller in September 1999. Fifteen East Lancs Spryte bodied Volvo B6BLE saloons were delivered over the summer. The second of the batch, V502EFR, is seen on its way to South Harrow Station on the 487. *Ian Armstrong Collection*

Five more East Lancs Spryte bodied Volvo B6BLEs arrived in April 2000. The last of the five was registered W521CCK which is seen blinded for the 487 to Willesden Junction. *Ian Armstrong Collection*

bands worn by the single-deckers were removed, in favour of plain red. It was also at this time that the buses were given fleet numbers, these being VS501-19/21. Three additional East Lancs Spryte bodied Volvo B6BLEs were taken into stock by Metropolitan in April 2002. These followed on as VS522 to VS524 (LR02BNZ, EHH/J).

The Metropolitan Omnibus operation came to an end on 1 November 2002. On this date the routes and vehicles passed to the control of F E Thorpe of Wembley. The Thorpe name began to appear on the Volvos, along with a yellow cantrail. Thorpe lost the contracts for the 187 and 487 in March 2004, the routes passing to First London. At this time the Volvos were returned to Yorkshire Traction and redistributed around their operations.

DENNIS ARROW

CAPITAL CITYBUS

The first Dennis Arrows arrived with Capital Citybus in the autumn of 1996, these carrying Northern Counties Palatine II bodywork. Numbered 401 to 412, these buses were originally registered P901-12HMH. 401-4 arrived in September, followed by 405-12 in October. The first three wore the standard yellow Capital Citybus livery, whilst 404 to 412 were delivered in an orange and white livery for use on the East London Line rail replacement service. These were initially allocated to Northumberland Park, before moving to Hackney garage in October 1996. When they were less than a year old, this fleet of dozen double-deckers were re-registered P401-12PLE in May 1997.

Four more arrived in December, following on as 413 to 416 (P413-6MTW). These were purchased from dealer stock and were also initially allocated to Hackney. They also saw service at Dagenham and Northumberland Park as required.

The first of thirty-eight East Lancs Pyoneer bodied Dennis Arrow double-deckers were delivered to Capital Citybus in 1997. Nine were taken into stock for the take up of route 369 (Ilford–Thames View Estate). These were numbered 417 to 425 (P417-25PVW), with 420/2/3 arriving in April, the others in May. All nine were allocated to Dagenham for the route. They were joined by another solitary Dennis Arrow in November. It followed on as 426 (R426SOY), the bus being exhibited at the Bus & Coach Show 1997.

Twenty-six arrived at Northumberland Park in the first eight months of 1998. Allocated rolling stock numbers 427 to 452, these buses were used on routes 76 (Waterloo–Northumberland Park Station) and 259 (Kings Cross–Edmonton Green)., along with night service N20 between Barnet Church and Trafalgar Square. Registration marks R427-43ULE, R844YLC, R445-50ULE, S451/2SLL were carried by these buses which were numbered 427 to 452 by Capital Citybus. The first arrived in April 1998 (427/9-36/8); with 437 and 446 putting in an appearance in May. 428/39-45/7-50 were all delivered to Capital Citybus in June. 452 arrived in July. 451 was the last to arrive, being taken into stock in August. Both the 76 and 259 penetrated into central London, meaning that these buses were required to wear the 80 per cent red livery, Capital Citybus' version being red with yellow and white.

The final Dennis Arrows to arrive were allocated to Dagenham in July 1998. These followed on as 453 and 454 (S453/4SLL), working alongside the earlier Dennis Arrows at that garage.

The East London Line contract ceased in the spring of 1998, the five Arrows operating in orange were repainted yellow. They were then allocated to either Dagenham or Hackney until withdrawal, this taking place between 2001 and 2004. In July 1998 410 sustained accident damage when it was hit from behind by a lorry. It returned to service wearing the 80 per cent red and yellow livery.

413/4/6 left London in 2002, with 415 remaining at Northumberland Park until 2004, being used on a school contract until this time. After their time in London, 401 to 416 were all cascaded to either First Leeds or First Manchester for further service.

Those used on the 76 and 259 (417-54) remained in service until 2003, at which time they were replaced by low-floor double-deckers, the 76 passing to Arriva London at this time. Initially moving south to First Hampshire & Dorset and First Somerset & Avon, they migrated north to First Manchester.

406
Gants Hill South Woodford
Walthamstow Tottenham Hale
Bruce Grove Turnpike Lane
123
WOOD GREEN
NICOS & CO
SOLICITORS
081 886 1166
KEBABS
BURGERS
PIZZA
152
First
P406 PLE
TURNPIKE LANE STATION
444
ARRIVA

VICTORIA
BUILDINGS
Catford Forest Hill
East Dulwich
185
LEWISHAM
419
...ONCE YOU'RE ON,
YOU'LL WANT TO GET OFF...
BOAT TRIP
IN CINEMAS FROM
OCTOBER 4TH
Victoria
ESPRESSO
DENNIS
First
P419 PVW

***Above*: A more** sizable fleet of twenty-six Dennis Arrows arrived in 1998. 432 (R432ULE) is photographed near Trafalgar Square shortly before terminating on the 91. *Ian Armstrong Collection*

***Opposite top*: The first** Dennis Arrows entered service with Capital Citybus in the autumn of 1996. 406 (P406PLE) was originally registered P906HMH. It is seen wearing the yellow livery of Capital Citybus whilst heading towards Wood Green on the 123. *Ian Armstrong Collection*

***Opposite bottom*: A third** consignment of Dennis Arrows arrived in the first part of 1997. 419 (P419PVW) is seen wearing the 80 per cent red livery applied to the Capital Citybus fleet. It is seen at Victoria at the start of its journey to Lewisham. *Ian Armstrong Collection*

442 (R442ULE) is another of the twenty-six-strong fleet of Dennis Arrows delivered in 1998. It is seen heading towards King's Cross on the 259. *Ian Armstrong Collection*

LONDON & COUNTRY

Ten East Lancs bodied Dennis Arrows were purchased by London & Country, arriving in April and May 1996. They were used on the 405 (West Croydon–Crawley), 410 (Reigate–Oxted) and 727 (London Heathrow Airport–Gatwick Airport). Registered N801-10TPK, these were numbered AD1-10. AD1-6 were allocated to Crawley, whilst AD7 and AD8 found homes at Merstham, being joined there by AD9 and AD10. The latter two vehicles were fitted with dual-purpose seating, being used by the Countryliner division of London & Country.

Passing to the Cowie Group, and later Arriva, the latter owner made heavy withdrawals in Surrey and Sussex. The Dennis Arrows moved to Arriva Yorkshire in 1999.

LONDON TRAVELLER

London Traveller purchased as a solitary East Lancs bodied Dennis Arrow in April 1998. The bus in question was registered R1LTB and was used by the company on rail replacement work, school contracts in the Barnet area, as well as routes 584 and 585 in the St Albans and Potters Bar areas. The transition of the company to the Metropolitan Omnibus Company saw R1LTB retained by London Traveller for use in the Watford area. It left the company in 2000, passing to Northamptonshire independent Rodgers of Weldon.

Ten East Lancs bodied Dennis Arrows were purchased by London & Country, primarily for use on routes 405, 410 and 727. However, AD06 (N806TPK), is photographed operating a journey on the 420, showing off its smart East Lancs bodywork. *Mike Harris*

VOLVO B7L & B7LA

GO AHEAD LONDON

A solitary Volvo B7L saloon featuring the Wright Eclipse body style was taken into stock by London Central at Bexleyheath in February 2002. Registered LF51CYC this saloon was numbered VWL1. It was put to use on the 486 between Bexleyheath and North Greenwich station, working alongside the fleet of East Lancs Myllennium bodied DAF SB220 MD-class. It remained on the route until July 2007, the 486 receiving a fleet of Enviro 400 double-deckers at this time.

The shuttle service between Luton Airport Parkway Station and Luton Airport was taken over by Go Ahead London from First Essex Buses on 7 December 2014. Whilst this operation is not in the TfL area, it is included here for completeness. From this date, a base close to the railway station was established by Go Ahead London who gave it the old London Transport garage code 'LS'. Five buses were acquired with the operation. This included a solitary Wright Eclipse bodied Volvo B7L saloon registered Y186HNH. It was officially numbered by Go Ahead as LUT5 but also carried its former First Essex fleet number 66358. Fleet numbers LUT1 to LUT4 were allocated to four Volvo B7LA articulated buses operating on the same route. The first three (LUT1-3) carried Wright Eclipse Fusion bodywork. These were registered T3/4/5FCC, originating as WX55HWF/G/H. Like LUT5, these also carried their former First Essex fleet numbers 10180 to 10182. LUT4 (T6FCC) carried the more unusual Wright Streetcar body work. They operated the route until March 2023, being withdrawn following the opening of a monorail between the Airport and the Parkway station.

FIRST LONDON

First London was the only other operator to use the Volvo B7LA. Like the Go-Ahead London examples, these also carried Wright Eclipse Fusion bodywork. The first example of this type to operate in London was First Hampshire 136 (X36FPO). This bus was lent to First CentreWest for two days in mid-June 2001. It was tested along Uxbridge Road, as well as being used on test in Central London, running over Red Arrow services 507 and 521. Two similar buses, Y151 / 2ROT, arrived in September, these taking up fleet numbers AV1 and AV2 with First London. AV1 was loaned from First Southampton, whilst AV2 joined it from First Glasgow. The pair worked on the 207, operating alongside the four Volvo B10LA articulated buses mentioned earlier in this book. Like the B10LAs, these also left First London in May 2002, transferring to First Manchester for further use.

London Central took stock of a solitary Volvo B7L saloon in February 2002. Registered LF51CYC this bus took up rolling stock number VWL1. It is seen loading in Bexleyheath town centre before heading to North Greenwich Station on route 486. *Ian Armstrong Collection*

Luton Airport
Parkway Station
London Luton Airport
Luton Airport Parkway
Up to every 10 minutes
Trains from Luton Airport Parkway to:
Central London • Croydon •
• Sutton • Brighton • Bedford
T4 FCC

London Luton Airport
Trains from Luton Airport Parkway to:
Central London • Croydon •
• Sutton • Brighton • Bedford
T6 FCC

Above: **LUT5 (Y186HNH)** was a third type inherited by Go-Ahead London from First Essex in December 2014. This Wright Eclipse bodied Volvo B7L saloon is seen on its way to Luton Airport whilst carrying a heavy load. *Liam Farrer-Beddall*

Opposite top: **Go-Ahead London** took over the Luton Airport Parkway Station to Luton Airport shuttle service from First Essex in December, inheriting five buses with the service. These buses were given classification code LUT by their new owners, although these numbers were never carried. LUT2 (T4FCC) was one of a trio of Wright Eclipse Fusion bodied Volvo B7LAs taken over. It is seen heading along Airport Way, Luton on its way to the Airport. A special purple livery with route branding was applied to these saloons as can be seen. *Liam Farrer-Beddall*

Opposite bottom: **LUT4 (T6FCC)** was the only Wright StreetCar bodied Volvo B7LA articulated bus acquired by Go-Ahead London with the Luton Airport division. It is also seen on Airport Way, Luton on its way to the Parkway railway station. The tunnel that goes under the taxiway can just be glimpsed in the background. *Liam Farrer-Beddall*

MERCEDES-BENZ CITARO

FIRST LONDON

First London was the first operator in London to take stock of the rigid Mercedes-Benz Citaro. Eleven thirty-six-seater Citaros were purchased by First London for use on the tourist service RV1 (Tower Gateway–Covent Garden). EC2001 was first to arrive in March 2002 carrying registration mark LT02NTV. It was joined by EC2002 to EC2011 (LT02NTX/Y, NUA/B/C/E/F/H/J, NVY) in April. Riverside branding was carried by these single-deckers. Hackney was chosen to garage these buses. A twelfth Citaro was added to the First London fleet in April 2002, being placed on long-term loan from London Buses. It carried registration mark LV02UUC and slotted into the fleet as EC2000. This bus was lent to Stagecoach London between April 2002 and March 2003, at which time it returned to First London. Little happened with these buses during their career with First London. They were renumbered in October 2003 from EC2000-11 to ES64000 to ES64011 respectively.

Three Fuel Cell Hydrogen powered Mercedes-Benz Citaros were taken into stock by First London in December 2003. These joined the other twelve at Hackney, initially being used on the 25 (Oxford Circus–Ilford Broadway) before joining the other Citaros on the RV1. Numbered ESQ64991 to ESQ64993 (LK53MBO/U/V) by First London, they carried branding to promote their alternative mode of power. The first two were exhibited at City Hall prior to entering service in mid-December. They were returned to Transport for London ownership January 2007, all three passing to various museums for preservation.

ES64005 was first to leave the fleet, passing to neighbouring First Berkshire in March 2008. The others departed London in 2011.

ES64006-11 were first to go, moving north to First Edinburgh in March. ES64001/2 were next to leave, joining ES64005 with First Berkshire, where they gained new registration marks OIG6491 and OIG6939. ES64003/4 were the last to leave London, being cascaded to First Scotland East in July 2011.

***Above*: Eleven Mercedes-Benz** Citaro saloons were purchased by First London for use on new route RV1 in 2002. The first of the batch ES64001 (LT02NTX), originally numbered EC2001, is seen having just crossed Tower Bridge on its way to Covent Garden. *David Beddall*

***Right*: ES64008 (LT02NUF)** is photographed having just crossed the River Thames using Waterloo Bridge shortly after leaving the Covent Garden terminus of the RV1. *Liam Farrer-Beddall*

Three hydrogen fuel cell Citaros entered the First London fleet in December 2003. These were originally trialled on the 25 before moving on to the RV1, operating alongside standard diesel Citaros. ESQ64991 (LK53MBO) was the first of these and is seen at the former Hackney garage. *Author*

EPSOM BUSES

Epsom Buses purchased seven Mercedes-Benz Citaro saloons in 2003 for use on the 293 (Morden–Epsom General Hospital). They were numbered MCL1 to MCL7 and carried registrations BW03ZMZ, BU53AWZ, AXA, AWY/X/W and BW03ZMY. MCL1 and MCL7 were delivered in August 2003, with MCL2-6 arriving in September. Quality Line lost the contract for the 293 to Metrobus from 30 August 2008. The new operator had ordered a fleet of Scania OmniCity single-deckers to operate the route. However, these were late in arriving, so MCL2-7 were placed on long-term loan to Metrobus. These were sold to Wealden PSV in August 2009. MCL1 was retained by Quality Line, and took new fleet number MCL30094 when the company was renumbered by RATP to fit in with London United and London Sovereign. It eventually left London in July 2020.

The X26 (Heathrow Airport – West Croydon) passed to the control of Quality Line in April 2012. Ten Citaros were ordered for the route, these being numbered MCL8 to MCL17. Registration marks BN12EOP/R/S/T/Y/V/W/X/Y/Z were carried by these single-deckers. They were used on the route until May 2017, at which time they were sold to Chartwell Bus & Coach.

BU13ZVE, a Mercedes-Benz Citaro K demonstrator found its way to Quality Line in July 2013. Numbered MBK1 it was used on routes 406 (Kingston–Epsom Clock Tower) and the X26 for the duration of its stay. This bus was used by many of the London operators as will be seen in this chapter.

A third batch of Citaros arrived with Quality Line in November 2016. They were put to use on the 413 (Sutton Garage–Morden Station) which the company had gained from London General. These

Route 293 received a fleet of seven Mercedes-Benz Citaros in August and September 2003. Just one survived with the company following the loss of the route in 2009. MCL1 (BW03ZMZ) was retained by Quality Line and is seen at Wiseley, attending the annual Cobham Bus Museum rally. *Liam Farrer-Beddall*

were the first and only Mercedes-Benz Citaro K saloons to operate in London. Stock numbers MCS01 to MCS09 were allotted to these buses which took up registration marks BV66GXY/Z, GYA/B/C/D/E/F/G. To help with type training, BU13ZVE was loaned for a second time in November 2016. This time it took up fleet number MCS10 for the duration of its stay. MCS01-09 were renumbered MCL30084-92 in July 2017.

Epsom Buses took stock of ten Citaros for the X26 in the spring of 2012. MCL15 (BN12EOX) is photographed paused opposite East Croydon railway station shortly before completing its journey from Heathrow Airport. *Liam Farrer-Beddall*

***Above*: Heathrow Airport** provides the backdrop to this photograph of MCL17 (BN12EOZ). The Citaros often suffered from capacity issues, the X26 being a popular route. On 15 April 2017 the X26 passed to Go-Ahead London, with the new operator using double-deckers on the route. *Liam Farrer-Beddall*

***Below*: Nine Mercedes-Benz** Citaro K buses arrived in November 2016 for the take up of route 413 from Go-Ahead London. MCS05 (BV66GYC) is photographed in Sutton town centre on its way to Morden. *Liam Farrer-Beddall*

The Citaro Ks also saw service on other Epsom Buses routes. This is shown by MCL30091 (BV66GYF) which is seen departing Cromwell Road bus station, Kingston on its way to West Molesey on the 411. These buses had been renumbered into the RATP London numbering sequence in July 2017. *Liam Farrer-Beddall*

GO-AHEAD LONDON

Go-Ahead London were by far the largest operator of the Mercedes-Benz Citaro. Excluding the articulated MAL-class, sixty-nine rigid examples were purchased by the company for operation in London, with four additional examples being loaned.

The first three hired Citaros arrived in July 2009 from sister company Metrobus. 503 to 505 (BU53AWY/Z, AXA) were used from Camberwell during the month for type training ahead of the delivery of fifty similar single-deckers for the Red Arrow services. 505 was returned to Metrobus the same month.

The fifty rigid Citaros replaced thirty-one MAL-class Citaro G articulated buses on the 507 (Waterloo–Victoria) and 521 (Waterloo–London Bridge). These were numbered MEC1 to MEC50 and were registered BG09JJK/L/U/V/X/Y/Z, JKE/F/J, BD09ZPR-Z, ZRA/C/E/F/G/J/K, BF59NHJ, BD09ZVT-Z, ZWA-C, ZWE/F/G/H, BT09GOH/J/K/P/U/X, GPE/F/J. MEC4, 20/2/4/5/9-31/4/6/9, 42/3/7 and MEC50 were all delivered in July. With the exception of MEC27, the rest followed in August. MEC27 was involved in an accident whilst on delivery and was returned to Germany for repair. It was delivered to London in September 2009, the original 09-registration mark that had been allocated to it surrendered in favour of the 59-registration mark shown in the list. Allocated to Waterloo, the weekend workings on the 507 were operated from Mandela Way. A number of the MEC-class were not used on the two routes at weekends, often finding themselves allocated to rail replacement work.

The Mercedes-Benz Citaro K demonstrator mentioned under the Quality Line heading (BU13ZVE) was lent to Go-Ahead London on three occasions. It was first loaned in September 2013 when it was used on the 355 (Mitcham–Brixton) from Camberwell numbered MBK1. It left at the end of the month, passing to Abellio London. It returned in August 2015 ahead of the new batch of Citaros due for the 358 (Orpington–Crystal Palace), operating with the company until November 2015.

The new Citaros for Metrobus' 358 arrived in September 2015. They continued the fleet numbering sequence on as MEC51-69 (BF65HUJ/O/K/P/U/V/Y/Z, HVA/B/C/D/E/G/H/J/L/ K/M). These were examples of the new Citaro 0295 model. A couple members of this batch of Citaros were incorrectly registered. This was rectified in January 2016 when MEC67 changed from BF65HVL to BF65HVK, and MEC68 from BF65HVK to BF65HVL. It was at this time that BU13ZVE made its third appearance with Go-Ahead London. It joined MEC51-69 on the 358, taking up stock number MEC70 when allocated to Green Street Green. MEC53 was renumbered MEC52 and MEC52 to MEC53 in November 2016.

MEC50 gained a commemorative red and white livery to celebrate fifty years of the Red Arrow network in April 2016. It was allocated temporary fleet number MBA50. It retained the livery until December, when it was repainted back into standard livery.

The MEC-class used on the Red Arrow network was replaced in 2016 by new SEe-class electric buses. The first were withdrawn in August, with others being taken out of service over the coming months. MEC1-7 were the first to be sent to Hants & Dorset Trim at Eastleigh for a refurbishment. The first two of these returned to New Cross in October. The same month saw MEC25 placed on loan at New Cross. MEC3, 4 and 6 all returned to London in November, again being allocated to New Cross. MEC5/7/8/9, 10/2, 20/7, 30/2/7 and 50 were also sent for refurbishment at the end of 2016. Those sent away were upseated from twenty-one-seaters to thirty-three seaters. Those at New Cross were used on the 108 (Lewisham–Stratford). MEC21, 42-5/7-9 left London in November 2016, passing to sister Go-Ahead company Carousel Buses in High Wycombe.

Fifteen of the early MEC-class Citaros (MEC11/5/6/7/9, 22/3/4/5/6/8/9, 31/3/9) were sent to Eastleigh for refurbishment and conversion to driver training buses. They retained their twenty-one-seat layout and received a new livery of ivory and purple. They were also used on rail replacement work at weekends. They were joined by MEC36 in February 2018 and MEC38 and MEC41 in March.

A new garage was opened at Morden Wharf, Greenwich to replace Mandela Way on 29 July 2017. From this date MEC1-10/2, 20/7, 30/2/4/7, 46 and 50 transferred to the new facility, from where they operated the 108.

MEC13, MEC14 and MEC18 transferred to Luton garage in October 2018 for use on the Airport shuttle service mentioned earlier in this book. Retaining their original seating layout, they were repainted purple to fit in with the existing fleet used on the shuttle service. MEC35 joined them at Luton in February 2019.

MBK1 (BU13ZVE) returned to Go-Ahead London in July 2018, leaving in December 2019.

Metrobus suffered a fire at their Green Street Green garage on 22 November 2018, with a number of buses being destroyed. Three of the Citaros used on the 358 were included in this, these being MEC54/6 and MEC60.

The remaining Citaros at Luton (MEC18, 35, 40) were withdrawn in March 2023. During this month a monorail service linked the Airport Parkway Station with Luton Airport itself, making the bus shuttle service redundant. The three Citaros were initially placed in store at High Wycombe.

Go-Ahead London took over the Fastrack network in the Dartford area from 10 November 2024. The company had purchased a batch of Irizar ie trams for use on the routes. However, these were delayed in entering service, resulting in a fleet of buses being sourced from Ensign Bus. Four 12m Citaros registered BX64WHH/J/K/L, formerly operated by APCOA at Luton Airport, were earmarked for use on the route, these being allocated fleet numbers MEC70 to MEC73. However, MEC71 never materialised with Go-Ahead London. MEC70/3 left the fleet in April 2025, with MEC72 following in May.

Route 358 was finally converted to the IE-class Irizar ie Trams, this being completed by January 2025. This led to the withdrawal and disposal of the MEC-class that had been used on the route to Carousel Buses. MEC62 was the last of these to operate on the route.

January 2025 saw the transfer of route 108 from Morden Wharf to New Cross, allowing the route to be converted to SEe-class electric buses. At this time, MEC7, 20/7, 34 made the move between the two garages. Some of the MEC-class that had been used on the 108 were transferred to the Fastrack operation at Dartford, replacing Enviro 200s on the route. Eleven examples moved across, these being MEC1-6, 8, 10, 12, 27, 32, 37, 46, 50.

***Above*: Fifty Mercedes**-Benz Citaro saloons were taken into stock by Go-Ahead London in the summer of 2009. Allocated to London General's Waterloo garage, they were used to replace thirty-one Citaro G articulated buses on the Red Arrow services 507 and 521. MEC17 (BD09ZPX) is photographed at Victoria bus station before starting its journey back to Waterloo. *Liam Farrer-Beddall*

***Below*: MEC26 (BD09ZRK)** is seen at the Waterloo terminus of route 507. The route shared this stop with the 211, the Enviro 400 behind being on this service. *Liam Farrer-Beddall*

Above: **Mercedes-Benz Citaro** demonstrator BU13ZVE was lent to Go-Ahead London on three separate occasions. Between August and November 2015 it operated with the Metrobus division where it was used on the 358. Numbered MBK1 it is photographed heading towards Crystal Palace on the 358 whilst passing through Bromley town centre. *Liam Farrer-Beddall*

Below: **Route 358** gained new rolling stock in September 2015 in the form of nineteen Citaros. MEC54 (BF65HUP) was numerically the fourth of the batch. It is photographed in Bromley South on its way to Orpington Station. MEC54 was one of three Citaros that were destroyed by fire on 22 November 2018 whilst at the Green Street Green garage. *Liam Farrer-Beddall*

Crystal Palace finds MEC66 (BF66HVJ), seen having completed its journey on the 358 from Orpington. It is seen blinded for its return journey. *Liam Farrer-Beddall*

2016 was the 50th anniversary of the Red Arrow network in London. To commemorate this, MEC50 (BT09GPJ) was given a special livery in April 2016. It is seen wearing this livery as it reaches journeys end on the 521 at Waterloo. *Liam Farrer-Beddall*

The conversion of the Red Arrow routes to electric buses in the second half of 2016 meant that the fleet of Citaros moved on to pastures new. Some of these were refurbished and moved to New Cross from where they were used on the 108 between Lewisham and Stratford. MEC2 (BG09JJL) was one of these and is seen in Lewisham town centre heading north to Stratford International. *Liam Farrer-Beddall*

Fifteen MEC-class Citaros were converted for use as driver training vehicles but could also be found operating rail replacement services. They also received a new livery of ivory and purple. MEC22 (BD09ZRE) is found operating a rail replacement service to Lewisham, about to pass through Orpington town centre. *Liam Farrer-Beddall*

Above: **Three Citaros** were transferred to the Luton garage in October 2018 where they supported the fleet of articulated Volvo B7LAs mentioned earlier in this book. MEC18 (BD09ZPY) was one of two that were repainted purple. It is photographed on layover at Luton Airport Parkway railway station. *Liam Farrer-Beddall*

Below: **Go-Ahead London** took over the contract for the Fastrack network in the Dartford and Gravesend areas of Kent. A fleet of Irizar ie trams were ordered for the service but a lack of infrastructure at the newly opened Dartford garage led to a delay in these buses entering service. As a stopgap, a number of Mercedes-Benz Citaros and Enviro 200s were acquired by Go-Ahead London for use on the routes. MEC10 (BG09JKJ) was one of the Citaros to be transferred. It is captured by the camera in Gravesend town centre wearing Fastrack branding. *Liam Farrer-Beddall*

LONDON UNITED/RATP LONDON

London United purchased seven Mercedes-Benz Citaro saloons in 2011. MCL1 to MCL7 (BD11LWN/O/P/R/S/T/U) were allocated to Hounslow when they arrived in August. They were used by the company on the 203 between Hounslow and Staines.

London United was another company to operate demonstrator BU13ZVE. It was placed on loan with the company in May 2013. Allocated to Hounslow Heath for use on the 116 (Hounslow Bus Station–Ashford Hospital) it was not used by the company until July, at which time it was used as a driver training vehicle. It soon left the company, only to return in November 2015. This time it was allocated fleet number MCS1, operating routes 110 (Twickenham–Hounslow–West Middlesex Hospital) and 203 from Hounslow. It left the fleet again in January 2016.

London United operated seven Mercedes-Benz Citaro saloons on route 203, these arriving in 2011. The penultimate member of the batch, MCL6 (BD11LWT), is seen parked at Hounslow before starting its journey to Staines. *Liam Farrer-Beddall*

MCL1-7 took up new rolling stock numbers MCL30301-7 in March 2016 when the London United and London Sovereign fleets were renumbered by the RATP Group.

The operations and vehicles of Quality Lane were officially transferred to London United's control from 26 June 2017. This led to the transfer of MCS01-10 and MCL01 to London United from this date. As mentioned above, these took up new fleet numbers MCS30084-93 and MCL30094 soon after.

A second renumbering of MCS30084-93 took place with these buses becoming MCM30084-92 at this time. The change in fleet numbers was done to denote the difference in length (10.6m), with other Citaros in the fleet measuring 12.0m.

STAGECOACH LONDON

Stagecoach made an unusual purchase in 2012 when the need arose to replace the rolling stock on the 227 (Crystal Palace–Bromley North). Twelve Mercedes-Benz Citaros were taken into stock in May to replace the fleet of aging Dart SLFs. Allocated to Bromley these buses were numbered 23101 to 23113. Registration marks LX12DKK/L/N/O/U/V/Y, DLD/E/F/J/K/N were carried. Like their predecessors, the Citaros remained true to the 227 until Stagecoach lost the contract to Metrobus in 2019, all twelve returning off lease by October.

Demonstrator BU13ZVE was loaned in February and March 2016 for various trials. It was placed under the care of both Bromley and Catford garages, returning at the end of March.

ABELLIO LONDON

Abellio operated demonstrator BU13ZVE during October 2013. It was numbered XMS1 by the company and was used on routes 235 (Brentford – Sunbury Village), 290 (Staines–Twickenham), 490 (Richmond–Heathrow Terminal 5), H25 (Hanworth–Hatton Cross), K3 (Roehampton–Esher) and R70 (Richmond–Hampton, The Avenue).

ARRIVA LONDON

BU13ZVE passed from Abellio London to Arriva London in November 2013. It was allocated to Ponders End for a couple of weeks where it was used on the 313 (Chingford Station–Potters Bar). It operated with the company until mid-December.

TOWER TRANSIT

BU13ZVE was numbered MV44701 for the duration of its stay with Tower Transit. Allocated to Lea Interchange it was used on the 444 (Chingford Station–Turnpike Lane Station). It was used by Tower Transit between July and August 2016.

Bromley town centre finds 23103 (LX12DKN) having just started its journey to Crystal Palace. Thirteen of the type were allocated to Bromley for use on the 227, replacing a fleet of Dart SLFs. *Liam Farrer-Beddall*

The last member of the Stagecoach London contingent of Citaros, 23113 (LX12DLN), is seen about to enter Crystal Palace bus station at the end of its journey from Bromley North. *Liam Farrer-Beddall*

MAN 12.240/14.240

METROLINE

Contract renewals in 2007 saw Metroline search for new buses. The first requirement was route 251 (Edgware Station–Arnos Grove), the new contract starting in May 2007. Eleven MCV Evolution bodied MAN 12.240 saloons were purchased for use on the route. These were numbered MM771 to MM781 (LK07ELH, AYC-H/J/L/M/N). MM771/2/4/6/7 arrived in March, with MM773/5/8-81 arriving in April. They replaced Dennis Dart SLF saloons on the route.

Five more arrived in August for use on the 206 (Kilburn Park Station–St Raphael's Estate). Fleet numbers MM782-86 were allotted to these single-deckers, which carried registration marks LK07AYO/P/S/T/U. Both batches were allocated to North Wembley, and were intermixed on the two services. Four more were added to the Metroline fleet in September, these continuing the numbering sequence as MM787 to MM790 (LK57EHX/Y/Z, EJA). These also saw service on the 206 and 251.

The final MAN 12.240 saloons were taken into stock shortly after. Eighteen arrived for use on route 90 between Northolt and Feltham, these being allocated to Perivale. Numbered MM810 to MM827, they were registered LK57AYD-H/J/L-P/S-Y. MM810-2/8/20 arrived in October 2007, followed by MM813-7/21/5/6 in November. MM822-4 and MM827 completed the delivery of the eighteen when they arrived in December. The registrations of MM787 to MM790 were swapped around in December 2007. This led to a renumbering of these four buses in January 2008. MM787 was re-registered LK57EJA, whilst MM788 to MM790 became LK57EHX/Y/Z.

North Wembley was closed as an operational garage in May 2009, the routes and buses allocated to it were re-allocated within the company. MM771-790 were transferred to Perivale where they were used on the 206. Route 251 itself transferred to Cricklewood. They also saw service on the 232 between St Raphael's Estate, Brent Cross and Turnpike Lane.

In November 2011 route 90 transferred from Perivale to nearby West Perivale. The MMs stayed at Perivale where they were used on route 70 (Acton–South Kensington) instead of Dennis Dart SLFs. This was a temporary measure and by January 2012 seventeen of the type had made the move to West Perivale where they were once again used on route 90. MM825 made the same move in February, with MM785 and MM823 following suit in April.

In June 2012, route232 was re-allocated to Cricklewood. It was at this time that the remaining MMs transferred to West Perivale, these joining others on the 90, as well as the E6 between Bulls Bridge Tesco and Greenford Station. Six MMs were retained at Perivale for use on the 70 until the route passed to First London later in June.

The early MMs (MM771-8/81) were withdrawn from public service and put to use as driver training vehicles in June 2013. Over the course of 2014 these buses were repainted all-red, relieved by white vinyls. Enviro 200s replaced another nine MM-class saloons at West Perivale in August 2013. These were used as reserve vehicles over the coming years as the need arose.

The remaining MMs were moved about during 2015. In July MM779/82-4 found a new home at Brentford where they were used alongside other types on the E8 (Brentford–Ealing), being joined by MM817/8 in August. Those that remained at West Perivale were withdrawn over the summer months of 2015. The E6 was converted to Enviro 200s and the 90 to double-deckers at this time. May 2016 saw those operating the E8 withdrawn from service, with MM785 being the last to be used in public service. Most were converted to driver training buses, being repainted in an all-over red livery.

The first MM-class saloons left the Metroline fleet in 2015, these passing to Sullivan Buses. Others left the fleet at various times between 2008 and 2023.

Metroline took stock of a number of MCV Evolution bodied MAN 12.240 saloons for a number of their routes in West London. The first was the 251, taking eleven of these buses. MM780 (LK07AYM) was one of the MANs that were taken into stock for the route. *Ian Armstrong Collection*

MM786 (LK57EHW) formed part of the second batch of MM-class MCV Evolution bodied MAN 12.240 saloons, this time taken into stock for the 206. It is seen heading towards St Raphael's on its intended service 206. *Ian Armstrong Collection*

Above: **Hatton Cross** finds MM818 (LK57AYN), one of eighteen MAN 12.240s with MCV Evolution bodywork to be taken into stock by Metroline for route 90. It is seen on its way to Northolt. *Ian Armstrong Collection*

Below: **The MM-class** could also be found operating on the 232. MM823 (LK57AYU) shows this when photographed at Brent Cross shopping centre on its way to St Raphael's. *Liam Farrer-Beddall*

Above: **As well** as the 90, the MMs allocated to West Perivale could also be found operating the E6 between Bulls Bridge and Greenford Station. MM779 (LK07AYL) is seen on its way to Bulls Bridge when captured by the camera at Greenford Broadway. *Liam Farrer-Beddall*

Below: **Nine of** the early MM-class were converted to driver training buses in June 2013. MM775 (LK07AYF) was one of those and is seen exiting Edgware bus station whilst on training duties. *Liam Farrer-Beddall*

FIRST LONDON

First London took stock of a solitary MCV Evolution bodied MAN 12.240 from MAN, Swindon in June 2008 for a three-month trial. Registered WX08SXU, this saloon was numbered 49000 for the duration of its stay. It was initially allocated to Willesden Junction before moving across to Dagenham in July. From this garage it was used on rail replacement duties for the Jubilee Line. In August it entered service on the 498 (Brentwood Sainsbury's – Romford Station). The loan was extended, and 49000 eventually returned to its rightful owner in December 2008.

METROBUS

Metrobus ordered five East Lancs Esteem bodied MAN 12.240 saloons to replace Caetano Nimbus bodied Transbus Darts on the R2 (Petts Wood–Orpington–Biggin Hill). These were numbered 701 to 705 (PN07KRK/O/U/V/X). They were due to have been delivered to Metrobus in December 2006 but were delayed until April 2007. The quintet soon suffered with faults, with two having to return to East Lancashire coach builders for rectification work. Three ADL Enviro 200 bodied saloons with a similar chassis were ordered for the T32, these too were late arriving. This led to 703-5 being used on the T32 from Croydon on a short-term basis.

Metrobus also took stock of a batch of MANs with MCV Evolution bodywork. 709 to 723 (AE09DHG/K, AJ58WBD, AE09DHM,/P, AJ58WBG, AE09DHU/N/L, AJ58WBK/F, AE09DHV) arrived between February and April 2009. They were used primarily on the 202 between Crystal Palace and Blackheath. These were late in arriving, being required from November 2008 but delivered between the dates mentioned previously. Scania double-deckers were used on the 202 until the MANs arrived. 709-23 were based on the MAN 14.240 chassis.

The temporary need for shorter buses on the 293 (Morden–Epsom Hospital) arose in the autumn of 2012, leading to a temporary swap of vehicles. Members of this batch were used on the T32 (Addington

Village–New Addington) and 130 (Norwood Junction–New Addington). 721 to 723 were swapped with Darts in September, moving short-term to Crawley where they were used on the 465 (Kingston–Dorking).

Route 202 gained a fleet of double-deckers in September 2013. Some of the MANs were re-allocated to Green Street Green where they saw service on the 246 (Chartwell–Bromley North), with appearances on the 126, 181 and 284. Others remained at Croydon, forming a common user pool.

Three were put to use on the 359 (Purley–Addington Village) after the route was extended in September 2015, seeing an increase in the peak vehicle requirement from one single-decker to three.

The first of the type were withdrawn in October 2015, passing to Ensign Bus. Further withdrawals took place in 2017 and 2018, the last members of the batch leaving London in March 2019, being sold to Ensign Bus. These latter buses (709/13/15/7/8/20/1) were sold by Ensign for scrap.

705 (PN07KRX) was the last of five East Lancs Esteem bodied MAN 12.240 saloons taken into stock by Metrobus for use on the R2. It is seen having just passed through Orpington town centre whilst heading towards Biggin Hill Valley whilst operating the R2. *Liam Farrer-Beddall*

Blackheath Royal Standard
202
247
eVolution
713
METROBUS
MCV
AE09 DHP

Norwood Junction
130
METROBUS
eVolution
712
METROBUS
AE09 DHN

***Above*: The double-decking** of the 202 in September 2013 meant that the MAN saloons were put to further use by Metrobus. By this time the TfL services operated by the company had been transferred under the Go-Ahead London operation. Some were used on the 246, this being the route we see 709 (AE09DHG) on, photographed at the Bromley North terminus. *Liam Farrer-Beddall*

***Opposite top*: Fifteen MCV** Evolution bodied MAN 12.240 saloons were purchased by Metrobus for use on the 202. 713 (AE09DHP) is seen at Crystal Palace bus station before setting off to Blackheath, Royal Standard. *Liam Farrer-Beddall*

***Opposite bottom*: New Addington** finds 712 (AE09DHM) which was used on both the T32 and 130 in the autumn of 2010 following the need for shorter buses on the 293. *Liam Farrer-Beddall*

WRIGHTBUS ELECTROCITY

TRAVEL LONDON

Five Wrightbus Electrocity single-deckers were purchased by Travel London for use on route 129 (North Greenwich Station–Greenwich, King William Walk). The first three arrived in October 2007 registered LF07CCZ, CDE and CDK. LF07CDN and LF07CDO followed in November. Collectively they were numbered 8801 to 8805 by Travel London. Before entering service they were re-registered to LJ57YAY / X, YBA, YAW and YBB. Like other hybrid buses of that period they were adorned with green leaf livery. They were allocated to Walworth.

Travel London was acquired by Ned Railways in June 2009, later being re-branded as Abellio London. 8801-5 transferred to the new operator, continuing to be used on the 129. They were withdrawn from service in December 2012, returning off lease.

Five Wrightbus ElectroCity saloons were taken into stock by Travel London in 2007. The last of the five, 8805 (LJ57YBB), is seen operating a journey on the 129 to Greenwich, Cutty Sark showing of its green leaf livery. *Ian Armstrong Collection*

GO AHEAD LONDON

Go-Ahead London purchased thirteen Wrightbus Electrocity saloons for use on the 360 (Royal Albert Hall–Elephant & Castle). These were allocated to London Central's Camberwell garage.

The thirteen buses were delivered in stages. WHY2 to WHY6 were delivered between December 2005 and February 2006 carrying registrations LX55EAC/E/F/G/J. WHY1 (LX06ECN) followed in February 2006. A seventh arrived in January 2008 registered LX57CLZ, this following on from the others as WHY7. A couple of years passed before the final six put in an appearance. WHY8 to WHY13 (LX11DVA/B/C/F/G/H) arrived in August 2011. Green leaf livery was again worn by these buses.

The WHY-class experienced a number of problems but remained in service until 2018. WHY8 and WHY9 passed to Eminox for use as test vehicles in June. The others were sold for scrap in December.

Six Wrightbus Electrocity saloons arrived with Go-Ahead London between December 2005 and February 2006. WHY4 (LX55EAF) was one of the first to arrive. It is seen out of service passing through Victoria, wearing the green-leaf livery applied to the initial fleet of hybrid buses in London. *Liam Farrer-Beddall*

Six additional Electrocity saloons arrived in August 2011. WHY10 (LX11DVC) represents this batch and is seen at Elephant & Castle setting off on its journey to the Royal Albert Hall. *Liam Farrer-Beddall*

OPTARE TEMPO

EAST LONDON BUS GROUP/STAGECOACH LONDON

The East London Bus Group purchased five Optare Tempo hybrid single-deckers for use on the 276 (Stoke Newington–Newnham General Hospital). The first arrived in December 2008 registered YJ08PGO. This took up rolling stock number 29001 and was allocated to West Ham, being used as a type trainer. It gained new registration mark VLT14 in February 2009. The other four were delivered in May 2009. These followed on as 29002 to 29005 and carried registration marks LX09BGF/K/U/V. These single-deckers measured 10.6m in length and could seat twenty-eight passengers, these joining 29001 at West Ham. A special green leaf livery was applied to these buses to promote their environmentally friendly credentials. 29002 was re-registered to WLT461. 29001 lost its cherished registration mark in June 2010.

The East London Bus Group was purchased by the Stagecoach Group in October 2010, reintroducing the Stagecoach London name. Under their new owner, 29001-5 were renumbered 25111 to 25115. The 276 was lost to Go-Ahead London from 17 September 2011. After this date, the Tempos were transferred south of the river to Catford. From there they were used on the 380 (Lewisham–Belmarsh). They continued operating this route until March 2015, at which time they were withdrawn. They were sent back to West Ham for storage before being sold to Ensign Bus in April.

METROLINE

Metroline also took stock of five hybrid Optare Tempo saloons. They were allocated to Brentford for use on the E8 (Ealing Broadway–Brentford, Commerce Road). They were similar to the East London

Bus Group examples, being decorated in green leaf livery. OTH971 (LK58CTY) was first to arrive in January 2009. Allocated to the former Armchair garage at Brentford it was used as a type trainer. OTH972 and OTH973 (LK58CTZ, CUA) followed in February. The final pair followed in March, these taking registration marks LK09EKG/H, continuing the fleet numbering sequence as OTH974 and OTH975 respectively. They operated the E8 until withdrawal in 2014. OTH971/2 were first to leave London, returning off lease in April 2014. OTH973-5 followed in August.

LONDON UNITED/RATP LONDON

London United first operated an Optare Tempo demonstrator registered YJ59NNZ. Wearing a silver and blue livery, this bus arrived with the company towards then end of February 2011. This

Five Optare Tempo hybrid saloons were taken into stock by the East London Bus Group for the 276 in 2008/2009. These buses were added to the Stagecoach London fleet in October 2010 when the East London and Selkent operations were sold back to them. Less than a year later, in September 2011, the 276 was lost to Go-Ahead London. After this they were moved to Catford for use on the 380. It is on this route that we find 25111 (YJ08PGO) passing through Lewisham on its way to Belmarsh wearing the green-leaf livery. *Liam Farrer-Beddall*

was used prior to the arrival of sixteen Optare Tempos that had been ordered for the H37 (Richmond – Hounslow Bus Station), these arriving later than planned. OT1 to OT9 were taken into stock in April 2011 carrying registration marks YJ11EHG/H/K/L/M-P/R. OT10 to OT16 (YJ11EHS/T/U/V/W/X/Z) followed in May. All sixteen were allocated to Hounslow garage. Other than straying off route, not much happened to these buses during their careers in London. They wore a plain red livery relieved only by white fleet names. The batch were renumbered OT30201-16 by RATP London in March 2016. They remained in use with the company until May 2019 when they were returned off lease.

Another five Optare Tempo hybrids were taken into stock around the same time as the East London examples. OTH972 (LK58CTZ) is seen at the Ealing Broadway terminus of the E8. The branding and green leaf livery applied to these buses is clearly visible in this view. *Liam Farrer-Beddall*

SORRY NOT IN SERVICE
Optare
YJ59 NNZ

Hounslow
H37
Optare
LONDON UNITED
YJ11 EHH
OT 2
DE 22
MOONST☆RS CAFE
Saigon
VIETNAMESE & PEKING

Above: **The RATP** London fleet was renumbered into a five-digit numbering sequence in March 2016. OT8 (YJ11EHP) gained new fleet number OT30208. It is seen having just departed Richmond bus station at the start of its journey to Hounslow. *Liam Farrer-Beddall*

Opposite top: **YJ59NNZ was** an Optare Tempo demonstrator used by London United at Hounslow garage in early 2011. It is seen on the forecourt of Hounslow garage during its time with the company. *Liam Farrer-Beddall*

Opposite bottom: OT2 (YJ11EHH) arrived with London United in April 2011 for use on the H37. It is seen in Hounslow town centre shortly before reaching the Hounslow bus station terminus. *Liam Farrer-Beddall*

WRIGHTBUS GEMINI 2 INTEGRAL

ARRIVA LONDON

Arriva London operated five hybrid integral Gemini 2 double-deckers on route 141 between Palmers Green and London Bridge. These were numbered HW1 to HW5 (LJ09KRG, LJ58AVG/K, LJ09KRK/N). HW2 arrived in January, followed by HW3 and HW4 in February. HW5 was the fourth example to arrive, doing so in March. HW1 completed delivery of the quintet in April, with all five wearing green leaf livery. Allocated to Wood Green they were used alongside the HV-class Wright Eclipse Gemini bodied Volvo B5LH on the 141. They remained in service until May 2014, returning off lease during this month.

Five Wrightbus Gemini integral buses were taken into stock by Arriva London for trials alongside a similar number of HV-class Volvo B5LHs. HW4 (LJ09KRK) is seen passing Turnpike Lane on its way to London Bridge on route 141. *Liam Farrer-Beddall*

FIRST LONDON

First London purchased both the hybrid and standard diesel Gemini 2 integral model, both measuring 10.4m in length. The hybrids were first to arrive, doing so in December 2008. These were numbered WNH39001 to WNH39005 (LK58ECV/W/X/Y/Z). They were allocated to Westbourne Park, being used on the 328 (Chelsea–Golders Green) from January 2009.

The four diesel buses arrived in the opening months of 2009. WN35001 and WN35002 (LK58EDO/P) were first to arrive in January, followed by WN35003 (LK58EDR) in February. March saw the arrival of WN35004 (LK09CZS). These were also used on the 23.

WN35001-4 were passed to Tower Transit in June 2013 when First sold their London operations. In May 2021, WN35002-4 were lent to RATP London where they were re-numbered WV40902-4. They were returned to Tower Transit in August 2021. These left London in December 2021, passing to Bolton-based Vision Travel. WN35001 had departed earlier, being used in Budapest in the summer of 2021, before returning to the UK in July.

GO AHEAD LONDON

Go-Ahead London took two Gemini 2 integral buses into stock at the same time as First London. The hybrid version was registered LX58CWJ and took up rolling stock number WHD1. The standard diesel model took registration mark LX58CWG along with fleet number WDL1. WHD1 was allocated to London General at Stockwell where it was used on the 196 (Elephant & Castle–Norwood Junction). WDL1 found a home at London Central's Camberwell garage, where it worked alongside WVLs on the 68 (Euston–West Norwood) and X68 (Russell Square–West Croydon).

WDL1 left London in March 2019, passing to sister Go-Ahead group company Carousel Buses of High Wycombe. WHD1 returned to Wrightbus in March 2012, before returning to London in September 2016, this time being used by Tower Transit who numbered it WNH35501.

Above: **Five hybrid** Gemini Integral buses entered the First London fleet in December 2008. WNH39005 (LK58ECZ) is photographed at Notting Hill Gate on its way to Chelsea, World's End on route 328. The green leaf livery can just be seen. *David Beddall*

Below: **First London** also took four diesel integral Wrightbus Geminis, these being used predominantly on the 328. Allocated to Westbourne Park they also saw service on the 23. It is on this latter route that we find WN35002 (LK58EDP), which is seen heading towards Westbourne Park at Marble Arch. *Liam Farrer-Beddall*

Above: **Go-Ahead London** also took an example each of the hybrid and diesel integral Geminis. WDL1 (LX58CWG) was the diesel version which was initially employed on the 68 from Camberwell. June 2013 saw WDL1 transfer to Merton and it is from this garage that it was used on the 280. It is photographed in Sutton whilst heading towards Tooting, St George's Hospital. *Liam Farrer-Beddall*

Below: **The hybrid** Gemini Integral double-decker taken into stock by Go-Ahead London carried registration mark LX58CWJ, this being numbered WHD1 by the company. It is seen on its way to Hampstead Heath whilst on diversion at Aldwych due to central London road closures. *Liam Farrer-Beddall*

OPTARE VERSA

LONDON UNITED

Optare lent a demonstrator Optare Versa to London United in October 2008, this being registered YJ58BZY. It was used ahead of the arrival of eighteen similar buses in December 2008 and January 2009.

OV1 to OV10 arrived in December registered YJ58VBA-G/K-M, with OV11-9 YJ58VBN-/P/T-V/X-Z following in January. These 10.4m saloons were initially delivered to Hounslow Heath for storage before being allocated to Stamford Brook for route 391 (Richmond–Fulham). These wore an all-red livery, relieved by yellow fleet numbers.

The operations and vehicles of NSL Services of Twickenham were acquired by Transdev on 16 November 2009. Included in the acquisition were seventeen Optare Versas. These initially retained their former NSL fleet numbers (OVL50-66), carrying registration marks YJ58PHY/Z, PJO/U, YJ09EZE/F, EYT-Z, EZA-D. At the time of takeover they were operating route 283, continuing to operate from the former NSL Services garage at Park Royal. These were also 10.4m long single-deckers, and in June 2010 they were renumbered OV50 to OV66.

OV1 to OV18 transferred to Fulwel in May 2014, with OV19 moving to Park Royal where it continued operating the 391. A couple of months later, in July, OV1-11 were transferred from Fulwell to Park Royal, being joined there by OV13 and OV15. The transfer was due to the closure of Putney Bridge.

In March 2016 the London United and London Sovereign fleets were renumbered into a five-digit service. The Optare Versas were renumbered OV30101-19 and OV30150-66.

January 2019 saw the first withdrawals of the type. The majority of OV30101-16 were returned off lease in March, with OV30110/1/7/8/9 departing the capital in August, with OV30150-66 also returning off lease during August.

EAST LONDON BUS GROUP/STAGECOACH LONDON

Optare demonstrator YJ58BZY was lent to the East London Bus Group at Plumstead in January 2009, being used to help with driver familiarisation duties.

The first nine Versas were delivered to the Selkent division of the East London Bus Group in February 2009. 37001 to 37009 (LX58CHF/G/H/J/K/L/N/O/V) were allocated to Plumstead from where they entered service on the 469 (Queen Elizabeth Hospital–Erith). 37010-4 arrived in March carrying registration marks LX09AAE/F/J/K/N. They joined the East London fleet at Barking. These were used on the 369 (Ilford–Thames View Estate). Those at Plumstead were late in arriving, their place on the 469 being covered by Dennis Dart SLFs until their arrival.

It was found that 37011 and 37013 had conflicts with their registration marks and chassis numbers. To rectify this, the pair swapped identities in May 2009.

East London Bus Group was purchased by Stagecoach in October 2010. 37001-14 were renumbered 25301 to 25314 by their new owners.

25301 to 25304 were withdrawn from passenger service in March 2016 and were used by Stagecoach as driver training vehicles. 25305 was also converted to a driver training vehicle in June 2016.

Withdrawal of the fourteen Versas was drawn out. 25306-9 were withdrawn and sold in March 2017, followed by 25312 in May. 25301 was scrapped in September 2018. Others lasted until November (25304) or December 2019 (25310/1/3/4). 25302/3/5 were last to be withdrawn, these lasting until the spring of 2021.

NCP CHALLENGER/NSL SERVICES, TWICKENHAM

In the spring of 2009 seventeen Optare Versas were taken into stock by NCP Challenger of Twickenham. Numbered OVL50 to OVL66

(YJ58PHY/Z, PJO/U, YJ09EZE/F, EYT-Z, EZA-D) they were used on the 283 (East Acton–Barnes). OVL50-2 arrived in February, the rest arriving in March, these being allocated to Park Royal. The 283 was taken over by NCP Challenger from 28 February 2009, the route being operated by DPS-class Dennis Dart SLF single-deckers loaned from Transdev London. Little of interest happened to these buses during their short service with NCP Challenger and NSL Services. On 16 November 2009, NSL Services, as NCP Challenger had become by this time, passed their TfL services and vehicles to London United, as mentioned above. OVL50-66 transferred to London United at this time, with details listed under that heading above.

EPSOM BUSES (QUALITY LINE)

Quality Line won the contract for the 411 in 2010, taking it on from London United. Eight Optare Versas were purchased for use on the route. These were numbered OV01 to OV08 and were registered YJ60KGA/E/F/G/K/N/O/P. All eight were delivered to the company during October 2010.

Five more were purchased by the company when they took over route 465 (Kingston–Dorking) from Metrobus on 30 June 2012. These followed on as OV09 to OV13 (YJ12PKV/X/Y/Z). All five were taken into stock before the route was taken over.

Another Versa was used by Quality Line. The vehicle concerned was registered OP07ARE and had been used by Go-Ahead London prior to it operating with Quality Line. Arriving in November 2015, it entered service in December on routes 406, 418, 465 and X26. It retained fleet number HOV1, and was used to cover for OV03 which had suffered accident damage. In April 2017 it was renumbered OMH25006, leaving Quality Line in 2018.

Quality Line's original Versas, OV01-13, were renumbered into the RATP London fleet numbering sequence in April 2017. They took up new rolling stock numbers OV30071-83.

GO AHEAD LONDON

Just one Optare Versa was operated by Go-Ahead London. Hybrid demonstrator OP07ARE was lent to the company from 10 August 2011. Numbered HOV1 it was allocated to London Central at Camberwell who used this bus on the 360 alongside the WHY-class ElectroCity single-deckers. It was used until October 2012 when it left the fleet.

London United converted route 391 to Optare Versa operation in 2009. OV11 (YJ58VBN) is seen on its way to Fulham travelling around the one-way system that circles Hammersmith bus station. *Liam Farrer-Beddall*

Above: **OV54 (YJ09EZE)** represents the fleet of seventeen Optare Versas that were inherited by London United from NSL Services in November 2009. It is photographed at Shepherds Bush Green on its way to Barnes on route 283. *Liam Farrer-Beddall*

Below: **37001 (LX58CHF)** was one of nine Optare Versa saloons to be allocated to Plumstead garage for use on the 469. Purchased by the East London Bus Group it is seen passing North Woolwich station on its way to the Queen Elizabeth Hospital. *David Beddall*

Above: **Ilford Broadway** finds East London's 37012 (LX09AAJ), one of five Optare Versa saloons purchased by the company for use on the 369. *Liam Farrer-Beddall*

Below: **Woolwich town** centre finds Stagecoach London's 25304 (LX58CHJ), originally 37004 with the East London Bus Group. Woolwich Arsenal station can be viewed in this photograph. *Liam Farrer-Beddall*

Above: **Seventeen Optare** Versas were purchased by NCP Challenger, later becoming NSL Services of Twickenham. These were employed on the 283. OVL56 (YJ09EYT) is seen paused at the lower bus station at Hammersmith. *Liam Farrer-Beddall*

Below: **Eight Optare** Versa saloons were purchased in 2010 for use on the 411. The penultimate member of the batch, OV07 (YJ60KGO), is seen departing Cromwell Road bus station, Kingston on the start of its journey to West Molesey on the 411. *Liam Farrer-Beddall*

Above: **Five additional** Optare Versas arrived in June 2012, this time for use on the 465 between Kingston and Dorking. OV09 (YJ12PKV) is seen at journeys end in Kingston. *Liam Farrer-Beddall*

Below: **Go-Ahead London** operated a hybrid Optare Versa demonstrator alongside its fleet of Wrightbus Electrocity saloons on the 360 for just over a year in 2011/2012. Registered OP07ARE, it took up fleet number HOV1 and operated from Camberwell garage. It was also used in 2015 by Quality Line who also used fleet number HOV1. It is seen operating with Go-Ahead London when photographed at Elephant & Castle. *Liam Farrer-Beddall*

WRIGHTBUS STREETLITE WF/DF

The Streetlite is an integral single-deck introduced by Wrightbus of Ballymena in 2010. Originally only available as the WF model (wheel forward), Wrightbus introduced the door forward model (DF) in 2011, followed by the Max model in 2012.

FIRST LONDON

First London operated just one Wrightbus Streetlite, a door forward model. This was a demonstrator registered DRZ6181. It was allocated fleet number 47400 for the duration of its stay. 47400 was taken into stock by the company in December 2011 and allocated to Willesden Junction. From there it was used on the 226 (Golders Green–Ealing Broadway).

GO AHEAD LONDON

Go-Ahead London was the first operator to use the Streetlite to convert a route. The company took stock of both the WF and DF model which were both classified WS. Go-Ahead was the only London operator to take stock of the WF model from new, others listed taking second-hand models. The Go-Ahead London Group was made up of London Central, London General, Blue Triangle, Docklands Buses and Metrobus.

On 24 March 2012, Blue Triangle took on the contract for route 462 (Ilford–Hainault). Nine 8.8m Streetlite WFs were purchased by the company for use on the route, these seating twenty-eight passengers. Allocated to Rainham they took up stock numbers WS1 to WS9 (LJ12CGF/G/K/O/U/V/X/Y/Z).

In the summer of 2013, twenty-three Streetlite DF saloons were taken into stock. Split into two batches they were all allocated to London General. Eleven 10.8m long DF Streetlites were allocated to Merton numbered WS10 to WS20, these carrying registration marks LJ13GJU/V/X/Y/Z, GKA/C/D/E/F/G. Initially stored at Belvedere, they were put to use on the 219 (Clapham Junction–Wimbledon). The second consignment totalled twelve. These were shorter than those used on the 219, measuring 10.2m in length. WS21-32 (LJ13GKK/L/N/O/P/U/V/X/Y/Z, GLF/K) were allocated to Northumberland Park where they used on the 491 (Waltham Cross–North Middlesex Hospital). WS10-7, 21-31 all arrived in May, with WS18-20, 32 arriving in June.

Another sixteen WFs were delivered to London General in January and February 2015. They were used on the 192 (Enfield–Tottenham Hale) from Northumberland Park. Fleet numbers WS33-48 (SN64CTZ, CUA/C/G/H/J/K/O/U/V/W/X/Y, CVA-C) were allotted to these buses. These were, however, a short-term measure and were replaced in July 2015 by similar saloons. These new vehicles followed on as WS49 to WS64 which carried registration marks SM15HWR-H/J/K, VJZ, VKA-E, WCK/L/N/O. WS49-57 arrived in July, with WS58-64 following in August. This latter batch were fitted with fly wheels, making them more environmentally friendly. Following the arrival of WS49-64, WS33 to WS48 were returned to Wrightbus for resale. A number of these returned to London service, passing to RATP London, further details of which can be found later in this chapter. Three of the original batch returned to Go-Ahead London in April 2017. WS35/6/8 (SN64CUC/G/J) were added to the Commercial Service fleet at Silvertown. From there they operated a contract between Stratford International, Stratford City and the HereEast campus, located in the Queen Elizabeth Olympic Park. Different liveries were worn by these buses for use on the contract, with WS33 sporting a dark grey livery, WS36 an orange and grey one, with WS38 wearing a turquoise and grey livery.

London Central took stock of its first Streetlite, a DF model, in July 2016. WS65 (SL16YPK) was acquired for evaluation purposes. Allocated to New Cross, this saloon carried a Mercedes engine and was used by the company on the 108 (Lewisham–Stratford City). Measuring 10.2m this single-decker could seat twenty-nine.

In October 2016 the rolling stock used on the 39 (Clapham Junction–Putney Bridge Station) was upgraded. Numbered WS66 to WS74, these buses carried registration marks SK66HSC/E/F/G/J/L/N/O/U, seated thirty-one and measured 10.8m.

The next four Streetlite DFs arrived in April 2017. WS75 to WS78 (SK17HFU/V/W/X) were destined for route 455 to partly convert the route to the type. However, these 10.8m long saloons were found to be too long to navigate the area around Old Lodge Lane. They were therefore allocated to Plough Lane to replace SE-class Enviro 200s on the 39.

Go-Ahead London lost the contract for the 462 in 2017 to Stagecoach London, with WS1-9 being made redundant. In May they transferred to Metrobus at Green Street Green, where they were used on local services in the Orpington area.

Northumberland Park received two more WF saloons in July 2017. WS79 and WS80 (SK17HHE/F) were put to use on the 379 between Chingford and Yardley Lane Estate. Six similar buses were allocated to Putney in August. These followed on as WS81 to WS86 (SK17HKA-F) and were used on the 424 (Putney Heath–Fulham). Four 10.8m long Streetlite DFs arrived at Plough Lane during August. WS87 to WS90 (SK17HKG/H/J/L), these taking up service on the 39.

A month later, in September, thirteen 10.8m Streetlite DFs were delivered to Metrobus at their Croydon garage. Numbered WS91-103 (SK67FKA/B/E/F/G/H/J/L/M/N/O/P/S) they were used on the 355 (Mitcham–Brixton).

The final deliveries for 2017 arrived in November. Thirteen DFs arrived at Stockwell during the month for route 170 (Victoria–Roehampton).

These were numbered WS104 to WS116 and carried registration marks SK67FMA/C/D/E/F/J/L/M/O/P/U/V/X. Fourteen had been ordered for the route, the outstanding member arrived in May 2018. This followed on as WS117 (SN18XZV).

Route 491 was lost to Metroline at the beginning of June 2018. This led to WS21-32 being returned off lease.

Go-Ahead London gained two routes from other operators in 2019. Route 227 (Bromley North–Crystal Palace) was taken over from Stagecoach London from 22 June. Thirteen 11.5m thirty-five seater Streetlite DFs were taken into stock in May. WS118 to WS130 (SK19FBO/N/L/J/G/F/E/D/C/B/A, FAU/O) were allocated to Metrobus' Green Street Green garage.

The second route was the 232 (St Raphael's Estate–Turnpike Lane Station), taken over from Arriva London on 3 August. Eighteen shorter DFs, measuring 10.8m, arrived in July for the take up of the route. These followed on as WS131 to WS148 (SM19KKN/L/J/H/G/F/E/D/C/B/A, KJZ/Y/X/V/U/O/N), all of which were allocated to Northumberland Park.

The 192 was lost to Arriva London from 9 November 2019 so members of the Streetlite WF batch allocated to the route (WS49-67) moved around the Go-Ahead London Group. WS57-9 moved to Metrobus' Green Street Green garage in February 2020. WS56 and WS60 both followed in August, with WS51-5, 61-4 being reallocated to Green Street Green in September. WS61-4 returned to Northumberland Park in March 2021. When operating with Metrobus, these midibuses were used on various routes within the Orpington area.

WS33/4/7/9, 41-3/5/7/8 returned to Go-Ahead London in May 2021 from RATP London. They were allocated to Metrobus at Croydon from where they continued to operate the 463 (Coulsdon South–Pollards Hill).

Plough Lane garage was closed on 24 March 2023. This meant that WS67-78 transferred to Putney garage along with route 39.

Route 355 moved from Green Street Green to Camberwell garage in September 2023. At this time WS91-103 were transferred north.

The loss of the 379 in November 2023 saw the pair of Streetlites, WS79/80, placed into storage. They were soon reinstated at Northumberland Park where they were used on other services.

WS87 made the move from Putney to New Cross garage in June 2024 from where it was used on the P4 (Brixton–Lewisham). It was joined by WS77 and WS90 in November, these also entering service on the P4. By March 2025 fifteen Streelites had been allocated to New Cross for use on the P4, these being WS67-78, 87/8 and 90.

The first nine Wrightbus Streetlites purchased by Go-Ahead London were examples of the WF model. WS7 (LJ12CGX) is photographed at Ilford Broadway shortly before completing its journey to Ilford. *Liam Farrer-Beddall*

Above: **Route 219** was the next service to gain a fleet of Wrightbus Streetlites, this time the DF model being chosen. WS14 (LJ13GJZ) was one of eleven purchased for the route and is seen passing through Wimbledon town centre on its way to Clapham Junction. *Liam Farrer-Beddall*

Below: **Northumberland Park** were allocated twelve Streetlite DFs in the summer of 2013 for use on the 491. WS27 (LJ13GKV) is seen at Waltham Cross bus station at the start of its journey to North Middlesex Hospital. *Liam Farrer-Beddall*

Above: **The opening** months of 2015 saw the delivery of sixteen Streetlite WFs for use on route 192. WS42 (SN64CUV) is seen about to enter Edmonton Green bus station on its way to Enfield. *Liam Farrer-Beddall*

Below: **WS49 (SM15HWE)** was one of a second batch of Streetlite WFs to be taken into stock by Go-Ahead London for use on the 192. It is photographed passing the entrance to Edmonton Green bus station whilst heading towards Tottenham Hale. *Liam Farrer-Beddall*

***Above*: Three of** the original 192 Streetlite WFs returned to Go-Ahead London in April 2017, these being added to the Commercial Service fleet. Allocated to Silvertown they were used on the HereEast contract between Stratford International and the HereEast Campus at the Queen Elizabeth Olympic Park. WS38 (SN64CUJ) is seen passing Stratford International wearing its dedicated livery. *Liam Farrer-Beddall*

***Below*: WS65 (SL16YPK)** is photographed passing the *Cutty Sark* just before approaching the end stop. WS65 was purchased by Go-Ahead London, evaluating the Mercedes engine that was installed on the bus. *Liam Farrer-Beddall*

***Above*: Route 39** was the next recipient of the Wrightbus Streetlite DF. Nine were taken into stock in October 2016. WS71 (SK66HSL) is seen having just crossed Putney Bridge shortly before reaching jouney's end at Putney Bridge Underground station. *Liam Farrer-Beddall*

***Below*: Four more** Streetlite DFs arrived with Go-Ahead London in April 2017, ordered for use on the 455. Proving too long for the route, these four were also allocated to the 39. WS76 (SK17HFV) is seen departing Putney Bridge for its journey to Clapham Junction. *Liam Farrer-Beddall*

***Above*: The loss** of the 462 in 2017 saw the first nine Streetlite WFs transfer to Green Street Green for further use. WS1 (LJ12CGF) is seen in Orpington town centre on route R3, shortly before completing its journey at Orpington Station. *Liam Farrer-Beddall*

***Below*: Putney's route** 424 was next to receive the Streetlite WF model. WS83 (SK17HKC) is seen heading towards Fulham having just crossed Putney Bridge. *Liam Farrer-Beddall*

Above: **Tooting Broadway** finds WS101 (SK67FKO) on its way to Brixton on the 355. Thirteen DF saloons were allocated to Croydon for use on the route. *Liam Farrer-Beddall*

Below: **Another thirteen** DFs arrived in November 2017. WS105 (SK67FMC) is seen in Lewisham operating route 225 to Hither Green. *Liam Farrer-Beddall*

***Above*: The fourteenth** member of the 2017 batch did not arrive until May 2018. This took up rolling stock number WS117 (SN18XZV) and is seen in Erith whilst operating the 286 to Queen Mary's Hospital. *Liam Farrer-Beddall*

***Below*: WS129 (SK19FAU)** is the penultimate member of thirteen Streetlite DFs delivered to Go-Ahead London in 2019 for the take up of route 227. It is seen about to enter Crystal Palace bus station having completed its journey from Bromley North. *Liam Farrer-Beddall*

UNDERGROUND
Turnpike Lane Station 232
WS135
SM19 KKG

Chislehurst R7
Go Ahead London
R7 Chislehurst
WS55
SM15 VJZ

Above: **A pair** of Streetlite WFs arrived at Northumberland Park in July 2017 for use on the 379. The route was lost in November 2023; the pair being retained at Northumberland Park. The second one of the pair, WS80 (SK17HHF), is seen on route 456 to North Middlesex Hospital, passing through Enfield. *Liam Farrer-Beddall*

Opposite top: **The final** batch of Streetlites to be purchased by Go-Ahead London were employed on the 232. WS135 (SM19KKG) is photographed passing Wood Green Underground station on its way to Turnpike Lane. *Liam Farrer-Beddall*

Opposite bottom: **Additional Streetlite** WFs transferred into Green Street Green in November 2019 following the loss of the 192. WS55 (SM15VJZ) was one of those that made the move, and is seen in Orpington town centre. *Liam Farrer-Beddall*

METROLINE

Metroline took stock of a single 10.8m Streetlite DF in June 2015. It was allocated to Potters Bar for use on single-deck routes from that garage. It was numbered STL1470 for the duration of its stay with Metroline. It returned to Wrightbus in February 2016, seeing further service in London from 2018 with Sullivan Buses.

LONDON UNITED/QUALITY LINE/RATP LONDON

London United operated a single Streetlite WF. SN65OKM was taken into stock by the company in December 2015. Taking up rolling stock number WS1, the bus was allocated to Park Royal garage. WS1 was renumbered to WS20274 in March 2016. It joined other similar buses at Quality Line. WS20274 left the fleet in July 2019, passing to Vision Bus of Bolton.

It has been mentioned above that members of Go-Ahead London's original fleet of Streetlite WFs used on the 192 (WS33-48) were used

SN64CUW was new to Go-Ahead London for the 192 in 2015. After returning off lease, they returned to London service in early 2016 with Quality Line. Initially numbered WS07, this bus later taking up rolling stock number WS20270 in July 2016. It is seen on route 463 in Coulsdon. *Liam Farrer-Beddall*

Tower Transit's Westbourne Park garage was acquired by RATP in December 2021. Fourteen Streetlite DFs were added to the RATP fleet at this time. WLS30037 (SM68ESF) was one of these and is seen at Shepherds Bush on its way to Central Middlesex Hospital on the 228. *Liam Farrer-Beddall*

by Quality Line. Ten of these were acquired for use on the 463 (Coulsdon South Station–Pollards Hill). WS01 to WS10 (SN64CTZ, CUA/H/K/U/V/W/Y, CVB/C) arrived in January 2016. They were renumbered into the RATP London series in July 2016, becoming WS20264 to WS20273. They remained operating with RATP London until May 2021, at which time they moved back to Go-Ahead London who continued using them on the 463.

The Westbourne Park operation of Tower Transit transferred to the control of the RATP-Dev Group from 11 December 2021. This formed a new operator, Transit London. The transfer of this operation saw fourteen Streetlite DFs transfer. These were numbered WLS30027-30 (SN64CBS/H/J/L) and WLS30031-40 (SK17HGU/X/Y/Z, HHA/B, SM68ESF/G/N/O).

ARRIVA LONDON

Arriva London purchased thirty Streetlite DFs for operation in South London. The first twenty-two arrived in October 2016 registered LK66AMO/U/V/X, ANF/P/R/U-X, AOA-H/J/L-N. These were numbered SLS1 to SLS22 and found a home at Norwood. It was from here that they were used on route 450 (West Croydon–Lower Sydenham). The second batch arrived in the summer of 2017, following on as SLS23 to SLS30 (SK17HJF/G/J/N/O/U/V/X). In July SLS23-8 arrived, followed by SLS29 and SLS30 in August. These joined the previous examples at Norwood, being used on the 410 between Crystal Palace and Wallington. The 450 was lost to Go-Ahead London from 30 September 2023. The Streetlites from this service were transferred between September 2023 and January 2024 to Thornton Heath. They were used to replace the fleet of ENS-class Enviro 200 saloons being used on the 410. In April 2024 SLS26-30 were stood down after the full conversion of the 410, this route requiring seventeen buses. The fleet of Streetlites that were used on the 410 were refurbished over the summer of 2024. To help maintain a level of service, SLS22-25 were retained by Arriva. SLS27 and SLS28 were both returned to service at Thornton Heath during September 2024, being put to use once again on the 410. By November, SLS26 and SLS28 had been stood down, the latter vehicle being stood down for the second time in 2024. The same fate was experienced by SLS23/6/8-30 by the end of December.

SULLIVAN BUSES

On 3 February 2018, Sullivan Buses of South Mimms took up service on the 299 between Cockfosters and Muswell Hill. In January 2018 eight short 9.7m Streetlite DFs were taken into stock for use on the route. These were given fleet numbers SL90 to SL97 (CP, JF, JJ, KT, LW, MH, PJ, SL67SUL). A ninth Streetlite DF arrived ahead of the others in December 2017. It followed on as SL98 and carried registration mark SL15ZGR. Measuring 10.8m, this had formerly seen service with Metroline.

TOWER TRANSIT/STAGECOACH LONDON

Tower Transit took stock of their first Streetlite DF in January 2015. DRZ6181 had operated with their predecessor First London. This former demonstrator was numbered WL44700 by Tower Transit, who allocated it to Lea Interchange.

It was joined at Lea Interchange by WV46101 to WV46111 (SN64CVS, CVF/G/H/J/K/L/M/O/P/R). These were built to 10.8m and could carry thirty-one passengers. Arriving in February (WV46101/2) and March (WV46103-11) they were used on the 444 (Turnpike Lane Station–Chingford).

A second former demonstrator arrived with Tower Transit in March 2017. Like WL44700, DRZ4920 had also previously seen service in London, with Arriva London. Numbered WL44701 by its new owner, this 10.4m saloon was allocated to Lea Interchange.

Twenty 10.8m Streetlite DFs were ordered by Tower Transit for 2017 delivery to cover the takeover of the 236, and an increase in peak vehicle requirement on the W14. These were numbered WV46201 to WV46220 and carried registration marks SK17HFY/Z, HGA/C/D/E/F/G/J/L/M/N/O/P/U/X/Y/Z, HHA/B. These twenty single-deckers were delivered in May and June 2017.

A top-up for the 339 (Shadwell Station–Leytonstone Station) was needed towards the end of 2018. A solitary 9.7m DF model arrived in December registered SM68ERZ. This took up fleet number WM46001 and was allocated to Lea Interchange.

Four more followed in January 2019. These were numbered WV46221 to WV46224 (SM68ESF/G/N/O). These were longer DFs, measuring 10.8m. They were allocated to Westbourne Park for use on the 228 (Central Middlesex Hospital–Maida Hill).

WL44700 and WL44701 were both demoted to driver training vehicles in October 2020.

As mentioned earlier in this chapter under the RATP London heading, WV46101/4/5/7, 46215-24 transferred along with the Westbourne Park operation to the RATP Dev Group from 11 December 2021.

The Lea Interchange operation lasted six months more under Tower Transit control. From 25 June 2022, Lea Interchange, its routes and buses all passed to the Stagecoach Group, becoming known as the Lea Interchange Bus Co. Ltd. Stagecoach names and fleet numbers were applied to the buses. The Streetlites were renumbered 39121 to 39139 (WL44700/1, WV46103/6, WV46201-14 and WM46001). These continued to operate unaltered.

UNO

Uno Buses of Hatfield were no stranger to operating Wrightbus Streetlites. In 2012 six WFs were purchased to operate routes in Hertfordshire, with five more arriving in 2018 for use on a route between Bedford and Milton Keynes. An eleventh Streetlite, a WF model, was added to the fleet in August 2020. At this time, former Go-Ahead London SN64CVA was acquired by Uno who numbered it WS46. It was taken into stock to cover an increase in PVR on the 383 (Barnet, The Spires–Woodside Park Station) from 20 September 2020. It was also used to duplicate a school-time journey on the 395 in Harrow. An extension of the 383 to Finchley Memorial Hospital in October 2020 saw WS46 mostly used on this route.

***Above*: The fleet** of thirty Streetlite DFs purchased by Arriva London were all allocated to Norwood for use on routes 410 and 450. SLS3 (LK66AMV) is seen at West Croydon bus station on its way to Lower Sydenham on the 450. *Liam Farrer-Beddall*

***Below*: SLS26 (SK17HJN)** represents the 2017 delivery. It is seen entering Crystal Palace bus station having completed its journey on the 410. *Liam Farrer-Beddall*

The 299 was taken over by Sullivan Buses who employed a fleet of nine Streetlite DFs on the route. SL94 (LW67SUL) is captured by the camera at Southgate station on its way to Muswell Hill. *Liam Farrer-Beddall*

DRZ6181 had originally operated with First London and was the first Streetlite to operate in London. In June 2013 the First London operation passed to Tower Transit who acquired this bus in January 2015, giving it stock number WL44700. It is seen at Turnpike Lane having operated a journey on the 444 from Chingford. *Liam Farrer-Beddall*

***Above*: Eleven** Streetlite DFs arrived in the opening months of 2015. WV46108 (SN64CVM) is also seen approaching Turnpike Lane station having travelled in from Chingford. *Liam Farrer-Beddall*

***Below*: A** further twenty Streetlite DFs were ordered by Tower Transit for use on the 236. WV46215 (SK17HGU) is seen shortly before arriving at Finsbury Park Station. *Liam Farrer-Beddall*

***Above*: SM68ERZ was** a solitary Streetlite DF taken into stock to help top up the vehicle requirement on the 339. Numbered WM46001 by Tower Transit, this short 9.7m variant is seen at Mile End on its way to Shadwell. *Liam Farrer-Beddall*

***Below*: The final** four Streetlite DFs purchased by Tower Transit found themselves allocated to Westbourne Park, from where they were used on the 228. WV46221 (SM68ESF) was the first of the quartet and is seen at Central Middlesex Hospital. *Liam Farrer-Beddall*

***Above*: On 25** June 2022 Stagecoach took over the operations of Tower Transit's Lea Interchange garage, forming the Lea Interchange Bus Company. Nineteen Streetlites passed to Stagecoach including SK17HGF, which took up fleet number 39131. It is also seen on the approach to Finsbury Park Station. *Liam Farrer-Beddall*

***Below*: An increase** in the vehicle requirement on Uno route 383 led to the acquisition of Streetlite WF SN64CVA. It was numbered WS46 by the company and is photographed in Barnet on its way to Finchley Memorial Hospital. Route branding for the 383 was carried by this vehicle. *Liam Farrer-Beddall*

WRIGHTBUS STREETDECK

ARRIVA LONDON

Arriva London received the first Wrightbus Streetdeck double-decker in the Greater London area. Registered LK64DVV, this bus took up fleet number WS1 when it was delivered in January 2015. A month later it was re-numbered SW1. It was allocated to Wood Green.

Nine more were taken into stock for use on the 340 between Harrow and Edgware in July 2016. Initially operating on the Arriva the Shires operators' licence, these buses were allocated to Garston. They followed on as SW2 to SW10 (LK16BYB-D/F/G, BXJ/L/M/N). These were transferred to Arriva London. They continued to operate from Garston until the 9 June 2018, when Garston was closed. From this date the SWs moved to Palmers Green for continued operation. SW6 moved slightly earlier for driver familiarisation.

2018 saw the introduction of the hybrid electric Streetdeck HEV model. HW100 (SK68TNJ) was taken into stock at Norwood in September. It was compared against the Volvo B5LH on routes 2, 249 and 468. HW100 moved north to Palmers Green in March 2019 where it was mostly used on the 100 between Palmers Green and London Bridge. It was withdrawn in November 2019, leaving London in March 2020.

Arriva London lost the contract for the 340 from 2 September 2023, the route passing to RATP at this time. This resulted in the move of SW1 to SW10 from Palmers Green to South Croydon. They were initially put to use on the 312 (South Croydon–Norwood Junction) to cover a shortage of EMC-class Optare MetroCity single-deckers.

In June 2024 SW2-4 transferred out of London to sister company Arriva North West. These were put to use on rail replacement work for Merseyrail. They were joined by SW7 in August. SW1 was earmarked to make the same journey but remained in London.

GO AHEAD LONDON

London Central took stock of a solitary Streetdeck in February 2015. WSD1 (SN64CTV) was allocated to Camberwell from where it was used on route 12 (Dulwich Library–Oxford Circus). In November 2015 WSD1 moved to Bexleyheath where it remained until it left London in January 2017.

Twenty-two Wrightbus Streetdeck HEV96 double-deckers were taken into stock in May 2018. They were used to update the rolling stock on route 44 (Victoria–Tooting Station). Allocated to Merton

LK64DVV arrived with Arriva London in January 2015 numbered WS1. A month after its arrival it took up new fleet number SW1 as seen in the photograph. It is seen about to enter Edgware bus station whilst operating a journey on the 142 to Watford Junction. *Liam Farrer-Beddall*

they took up rolling stock numbers WSD2 to WSD23. Registration marks SN18XZU, XYV-Z, XZB-H/J-M/O/P/R/S/T were carried by these buses. The Volvo B5LH chassis was originally chosen for these double-deckers, but the order was altered to the HEV96 model in early 2018. The WSDs were also found operating on other double-deck routes from Merton.

WSD21 caught fire in late September 2023 whilst in service on the 44 at Victoria.

On 25 November 2023 route 44 moved from Merton to Stockwell. WSD1-12/4-20/2/3 also moved between these garages during the same month. WSD13 followed in December.

New to Arriva the Shires at Garston garage, SW4 (LK16BYD) was one of nine Wrightbus Streetdecks to transfer to Arriva London in June 2018 following the closure of Garston. It is seen at the start of its journey to Harrow bus station, exiting Edgware bus station. *Liam Farrer-Beddall*

September 2018 saw the arrival of another Wrightbus Streetdeck, this time a HEV model. Numbered HW100 (SK68TNJ), this bus was initially allocated to Norwood where it was compared against Wright bodied Volvo B5LH double-deckers. It moved to Palmers Green in March 2019 and was mostly used on the 141. It is seen on this route passing Wood Green Underground station. *Liam Farrer-Beddall*

WSD1 (SN64CTV) entered the Go-Ahead London fleet in November 2015. Originally allocated to Camberwell it moved to Bexleyheath at the beginning of 2017. It is in this latter location that it is photographed, blinded for its return journey to North Greenwich on the 486. *Liam Farrer-Beddall*

May 2018 saw the arrival of twenty-two Wrightbus Streetdeck HEV96 buses for route 44. WSD12 (SN18XZF) is seen travelling along Buckingham Palace Road, Victoria just before passing Victoria Coach Station. *Liam Farrer-Beddall*

Morden finds WSD22 (SN18XZS) operating a journey on the traditionally single-deck route 164 to Wimbledon. *Liam Farrer-Beddall*

RATP LONDON

RATP London took stock of a solitary Streetdeck HEV96 in 2018, this taking fleet number WH45252 (SK18TKY). Allocated to Park Royal, this bus was used on the 18 (Euston–Sudbury). It remained on the route until it returned off lease in December 2020.

TOWER TRANSIT/STAGECOACH LONDON

Twenty-eight Wrightbus Streetdeck HEV96s were ordered by Tower Transit for use on the 25 (Ilford–City Thameslink). These were allotted rolling stock numbers WH31101 to WH31128 and were registered out of sequence as SN68AGD/C/B/A, SK19FDO/N/M/L/J/G/F/E/D/C, SN68AFW/T/S, SK19FDA, FCZ/Y/X/V/U/O/N/M/L/J. WH31101-4/15-7 arrived in February 2019, the others following in March. These found homes at Lea Interchange garage.

Two of the batch were adorned with all-over advertisements during 2022. The first, WH31119 (SK19FCZ), was used to promote tourism to London under the 'Let's do London' campaign. In June, a similar advertisement was applied to WH31111 (SK19FDF). These were lost in July 2022 and December 2022.

On 25 June 2022 the Stagecoach Group purchased Tower Transit, this becoming known as the Lea Interchange Bus Co. Ltd. The Streetdecks were renumbered into the Stagecoach numbering sequence. They became 18901 to 18921 (WH31117/16/15/04/03/02/01 /21/20/19/18/14/13/12/11/10/09/08/07/06/05).

Under Stagecoach ownership, two more were given all-over advertisements. 18905 (SN68AGB) was given one for La'eeb in August 2022, this being replaced in October 2022 for MetaGedu. It retained this livery until August 2023 when it gained a third advertisement, this time for the £1.75 Hopper fare. 18917 also gained an advertisement for Let's Do London in May 2023, with 18917 carrying this advert until August and in October sister Streetdeck 18918 gained an all-over advertisement for Low Emissions.

HACKNEY COMMUNITY TRANSPORT (CT PLUS)

Hackney Community Transport took Wrightbus Streetdeck SN64CTV on loan from 25 March 2021 for a short while. This was numbered 2603 by the company, being the former Go-Ahead London WSD1.

Twenty-eight Wrightbus Streetdeck HEV96 double-decks were taken into stock by Tower Transit for use on the 25. WH31108 (SK19FDL) is seen departing Stratford bus station on its way to City Thameslink. *Liam Farrer-Beddall*

In June 2022 Tower Transit WH31111 (SK19FDF) carried an all-over advertisement for the Let's do London campaign. A month later the Lea Interchange operation of Tower Transit passed to Stagecoach London. WH31111 was renumbered 18915 by its new owner and is seen at Stratford bus station carrying this livery. *Liam Farrer-Beddall*

OPTARE METROCITY

QUALITY LINE

A number of Optare MetroCity saloons have operated in London since 2014. However, the majority of these single-deckers have been all-electric and there for will not feature under this heading. Fourteen diesel powered MetroCity single-deck buses entered service in the capital in 2014. A demonstrator registered YJ14BFY was lent to Quality Line from Optare Ltd in March 2014. Primarily used for driver familiarisation work ahead of a fleet of twelve arriving for route S1 (Mitcham, Lavender Fields–Sutton–Banstead). A month later, in April, it was used by Quality Line on school route 641, at which time it was allotted rolling stock number MCD01. This was an example of the MC990 model. In April 2014 this bus was also put to use on routes X26 and 467. It was later acquired by Quality Line to help cover extra work on the 465, officially being taken into stock during August 2014 when it was renumbered OM13.

The intended fleet of MetroCity single-decks ordered by Quality Line for use on the S1 arrived in May 2014, two months later than was expected. Fleet numbers OM1 to OM12 were allocated to these buses which carried registration marks YJ14BFA/E/F/K/L/M/N/O/P/U/V/X. Like OM13, these were of the MC990 model, measuring 9.9m in length. They displaced East Lancs Esteem bodied ADL Darts SD43-51.

A fourteenth MetroCity, this time being a MC1060 model and seating twenty-nine, was acquired by Quality Line from London United in March 2014. Registered YD63UZL, this bus took up stock number OC1 and was used mostly on the 411. Details of its brief operation with London United can be found below.

Control of Quality Line passed to London United on 26 June 2017. In July, the MetroCity saloons along with the rest of the Quality Line fleet were renumbered into a five-digit numbering system. OM1-13 became OM20227 to OM20239, whilst OC1 became OML20240. This latter bus was the first to be disposed of, passing to Go-Coach Hire of Otford, Kent in June 2019. Nothing of interest happened to these buses for a few years until 2021. It was announced at the beginning of the year that the Epsom operation of RATP London would be wound down and closed by mid-2021. This affected a number of routes including the MetroCity route S1, which was transferred to Go-Ahead London in July, with OM20227-238 passing to the new operator at the same time.

LONDON UNITED

As mentioned above, London United took stock of a diesel-powered MetroCity demonstrator in July 2014. Registered YD63UZL, this twenty-nine-seater was an example of the MC1060 model. Although it arrived at the beginning of July, it did not enter service until the latter part of September. It was used by London United on the H98 from Hounslow, operating the service alongside four similar electric MetroCity saloons which were given the OCE classification code. Its operation with London United was relatively brief, being withdrawn in January 2015, after which time it was stored until it was disposed of to Quality Line in March 2015.

GO AHEAD LONDON

On 3 July 2021, Go-Ahead London's Metrobus division took control of route S1 from RATP London's Quality Line operation. From this date, twelve Optare MetroCity saloons entered the Go-Ahead London fleet, being allocated to Croydon. Numbered OM2 to OM4 and OM6 to OM14, the registration marks carried were not in the same order as they were when operating with Quality Line, the order being YJ14BFF/M/A/E/N/P/L/V/K/O/U/X. OM20239 did not transfer to Go-Ahead London. Fleet number OM1 was used for an Enviro 200 (DE20022–YX09HJJ) which had been placed on short-term loan to Go-Ahead London from 3 July. Like their time with Quality Line, very little of interest happened to the MetroCity saloons. On 11 August 2023, route S1 transferred to Goat Road, Mitcham. However, the OMs did not transfer with the route, their place on the S1 being taken by SEs and SOEs. They found further work on the 455, operating alongside other types in the Go-Ahead London fleet. In March 2024 OMs returned to the S1 when it transferred back to Croydon.

Twelve diesel powered Optare MetroCity saloons were taken into stock by Epsom Buses during March 2014, these being used on route S1. OM08 (YJ14BFO) represents this small batch of buses. It is seen passing through Sutton town centre whilst heading towards Banstead on the S1. *Liam Farrer-Beddall*

Banstead
S1
QUALITY LINE
RATP GROUP
OM 20239
YJ14 BFY

Dorking
465
YD63 UZL

Above**: July 2021** saw the S1, along with the MetroCity saloons, transfer to Go-Ahead London. They were renumbered by their new owners, retaining the OM classification code. OM10 (YJ14BFV) is seen in Mitcham town centre having started its journey to Banstead. *Liam Farrer-Beddall*

Opposite top**: Another additional** Optare MetroCity arrived in March 2015. YD63UZL was longer than the original twelve. It took up rolling stock number OC1 until April 2017 when it was renumbered OML20240. It is seen heading to Dorking on the 465 when passing Fairfield bus station, Kingston. *Liam Farrer-Beddall*

Opposite bottom**:** YJ14BFY was a thirteenth Optare MetroCity that was acquired by Epsom Buses. This former demonstrator arrived with the company in August 2014 and was taken into stock to help cover the extra work generated on route 465. It is also seen in Sutton town centre on its way to Banstead. In April 2017 the batch was renumbered into the five-digit RATP London sequence, becoming OM20239. *Liam Farrer-Beddall*

BCI FBC6123BRZ5/BCI

Go-Ahead London trialled a tri-axle 12.5m long BCI double-decker on route 12. TA1 (LX18DGF) arrived with London Central in July 2018 at Camberwell. TA1 was imported by Ensign Bus on behalf of Transport for London. This was a hybrid double-decker, featuring air conditioning. It was stored at Ensign's Purfleet yard and entered service on 6 November 2018. It remained on the 12 until January 2023 when it transferred from Camberwell to River Road, Barking. It was used from the latter garage on school route 687. After a period in storage, TA1 was sold to Ensign Bus in July 2024.

The unique TfL specification BCI double-deck (TA1 – LX18DGF) is seen about to turn on to Whitehall, exiting Parliament Square whilst operating a journey on the 12 to Oxford Circus. *Liam Farrer-Beddall*

VOLVO B7RLE

GO AHEAD LONDON

Although not operated on TfL services, Go-Ahead London purchased ten Wright Eclipse Urban saloons in 2020. They were added to the commercial service fleet for use on rail replacement services. VWL45 to VWL48 (YX54FWL/M/N/O) were acquired from East Yorkshire Motor Services, arriving in January. They were joined by VWL49 to VWL54 (HF54HGG/O/P/U, HHK and HF05HXD). These were sourced from Go South Coast. All ten

Former Go-South Coast Wright Eclipse Urban bodied Volvo B7RLE HF54HGU was numbered VWL52 by Go-Ahead London. It is seen during a downpour at Bedford railway station whilst operating a rail replacement service between Bedford and Luton. *Liam Farrer-Beddall*

were officially allocated to Luton but were used where they were required. In March 2020, VWL47 was officially moved from Luton to Folkestone. In May 2023, Luton garage closed. VWL51-4 were re-allocated to the company's new premises located in Leighton Buzzard, Bedfordshire.

From the same source came HF05HXD, which took rolling stock number VWL54 with Go-Ahead London. The gaps in the perimeter fence at the former Luton garage allowed some good photography of the buses based there whilst not being used. This is the location of VWL54. *Liam Farrer-Beddall*

COACHES

The aim of this section is to provide a history of the coaching fleet operated by London Transport, London Buses Limited, London Coaches (up until 1992), and the privatised London operators who used coaches on both private hire, driver training and rail replacement duties.

LONDON BUSES LIMITED/LONDON COACHES

London Transport set up the Tours and Charter Division in 1984 in order to evaluate a coach. The coach concerned was registered B593XNO, this being a Berkhof Esprite bodied DAF MB200. Borrowed from Ensign Bus the coach wore a white-based livery, relieved by rainbow stripes.

In January 1986 a Mercedes-Benz O303 coach registered C778RJU was lent to Selkent at Plumstead. This silver-liveried coach was loaned for maintenance purposes from Yeates of Loughborough.

In 1986 the Tours and Charters Division was relaunched as London Coaches. The main interest of this operation was sightseeing work. However, the company also launched an express service between London and Birmingham, competing with National Express, under the name London Liner. Jointly worked with West Midlands PTE, the service was initially operated by three Duple Caribbean II bodied DAF MB230 coaches and a solitary Plaxton bodied DAF. The Duple bodied examples were registered C27-9MCX and took up rolling stock numbers DD7 to DD9. DP1 (B350CJX) was the Plaxton bodied DAF, with all four coaches being taken into stock during March 1986. However, DP1 was a temporary addition, returning to its leasing company at the end of March. DD7 was temporarily delicensed at the same time, leading to the loan of A382NNK, a Plaxton bodied Leyland Royal Tiger, operating with London Coaches until April. Battersea became the initial base for London Coaches.

In April 1986 a pair of Duple Caribbean Executive bodied Leyland Tiger coaches arrived. These took rolling stock numbers LD1 and LD2 which carried registration marks C766/7DYO. They were allocated to Battersea wearing a white livery relieved by colour bands similar to that applied to B593XNO. They were leased from the Stanley Hughes Group, a group from which London Coaches hired the majority of their coaches. In November, LD1 gained a red-based livery for London Coaches, and LD2 a white-based livery for private hire work.

The fleet on the London Liner service to Birmingham was upgraded during the summer of 1986. Four MCW Metroliners were delivered registered C101-4DYE, numbered ML1 to ML4. The first three arrived in May, with ML4 following in June. However, the service proved to be less popular than thought and was withdrawn by the summer of 1986. DD7-9 were put to further use by the company after the arrival of these double-deck coaches.

A second London Liner service was launched linking London with Eastbourne, with a pair of Leyland Olympian coaches being ordered. These were late in arriving which led to the use of DD7-9 on the route until they arrived.

A solitary MCW Highliner coach was loaned from MCW, Birmingham between May and July 1986. Registered ABM399A, it was allocated to Battersea in May before moving to Clapham in June.

The withdrawal of the London to Birmingham service meant that ML1-4 became surplus to requirements. However, they were retained for a while by London Coaches and lent to various operators. Of note, ML2 and ML4 were lent in April 1987 to Devon General, these returning in May when they were initially put up for sale, this later being cancelled. ML4 was placed on a three-month trial loan to Southampton City Transport in July. After its return, it was then placed on loan to United Automobile Services in December.

Another three Duple Caribbean bodied DAF MB230 coaches were leased form the Stanley Hughes Group in 1987. D291-3XCX (DD1-3) arrived at Battersea in April for use in the London Coaches fleet. A month later, in May, a Duple Dominant bodied AEC Reliance arrived from the same source. Registered AHE996T, it gained fleet number AD1. A fifth coach arrived in June registered C645LVH. This was another Duple bodied DAF MB230 which was numbered DD5 by London Coaches. This was also joined in June by a Van Hool bodied MB230 coach registered D133ACX (DV1), also leased from Stanley Hughes Group.

The original coach TC1 (B593XNO) was renumbered to DB1 in June 1987.

Another coach was taken on lease from Stanley Hughes in July. This time it was a Plaxton Supreme V bodied Bedford YNT. Wearing a white-based livery it was given stock number BP1 by London Coaches and carried registration mark TRA52X.

Further coaches arrived in September 1987, with five being leased from Stanley Hughes. These were the last vehicles to be taken into stock during 1987, all of which were allocated to London Coaches at Battersea. The first two were Van Hool Alizee bodied DAF SB2305, these being registered E312/3EVH and numbered DV2 and DV3 respectively. The other three were all based on the Leyland Leopard chassis, carrying Plaxton bodywork. Taking up rolling stock numbers LP1 to LP3 and registration marks GFV183S, KAD348V and PWK12W were carried by the trio.

In April 1988 the London Coaches operation moved from Battersea to Wandsworth. At this time AD1, AP2, DB1, DV1-3, DD1-3/5/7-9, LD1/2, LP1-3, ML1, 2, 4 crossed the river to the new base. AP2 (RPH622R), a Plaxton bodied AEC Reliance had been taken on lease from Stanley Hughes in February 1988.

Nine coaches were taken into stock in 1988, again all being leased from Stanley Hughes Group. The first four arrived in April registered E604-7LVH. These Van Hool Alizee bodied DAF MB230s were numbered DV4 to DV7 by London Coaches. Their arrival allowed four older coaches to be used on the company's commuter services from Dartford. The next three arrived in June. Numbered DD54, 60, 97 (E654KCX, E660XCX and D297XCX), these Duple bodied DAF coaches wore an all-white livery for use in the private hire fleet. The final pair arrived during September. Van Hool bodied DAF SB2305 D619YCX wore a silver-based livery and took up rolling stock number DV19. The other was a Plaxton bodied DAF MB230 registered D360PJA. It was numbered DP60 and wore a white-based livery.

1988 was a quiet year for the intake of coaches. A pair of Duple Dominant bodied Leyland Leopards arrived with the London Buses Limited operation in July. LD3 (OMA508V) and LD4 (OMA504V) were both sourced from Crosville Wales Ltd. LD3 was allocated to New Cross for use on private hire work, whilst LD4 was repainted into a blue and cream livery and allocated to the Bexleybus operation.

The first new coach of 1989 arrived in March numbered DV58 (F258RJX). It was joined in April by DV51-7/9/60 (F251RJX etc). Wearing an all-white livery they were used on tour and contract work. All were bodied by Van Hool, but the chassis models varied. DV51/2 were DAF MB230s, DV53/4/9/60 were DAF SB3000s and DV55-8 were DAF SB2305DHSs.

Further Van Hool bodied DAFs were leased from Stanley Hughes at the same time. DV8 to DV10 (F608-10HGO) were based on the DAF SB2305 chassis; whilst DV11-22 F611-22HGO were also examples of the SB2305 chassis (DV8/9, 13-7), SB3000 (DV11/2) or DAF MB230 (DV18-22). DV8-10 arrived in March, the others in April.

DD7-9 and LP3 were all returned to Stanley Hughes in April.

A pair of Plaxton Supreme IV Express bodied Leyland Leopard coaches were acquired from Cambus in May 1989. Originating with Eastern Counties they were registered JVF815/6V (LP5/6). The pair were allocated to Norbiton, replacing loaned vehicles. Kingston Bus and Coach names were applied to the vehicles.

DD97 (D297XCX) returned to the Stanley Hughes Group at the same time. A month later, former London Country Bus Services Plaxton Paramount 3200 bodied Leyland Tiger TP13 (A114EPA) was acquired from Kirkby Centre. It was allocated to London Forest at Leyton, being renumbered TP1 in August 1989.

Another coach to arrive from the Stanley Hughes Group was Duple bodied DAF SB2305 E654KCX, this being allotted rolling stock number DD54.

A pair of Plaxton Paramount bodied Leyland Tigers were allocated to Leaside in October 1989. Numbered TPL1 and TPL2 by London Buses, these vehicles carried registration marks G661/2WMD. Added to Leaside's private hire fleet, they were adorned with large Leaside Buses fleet names on the sides.

The final coach to put in an appearance in 1989 arrived with London Coaches in November. Registered C708HWC, this Berkhof bodied DAF MB200 was numbered DB2.

1990 opened with the delivery of two Plaxton Paramount bodied Leyland Tiger coaches in January. TP3 (G100VNM) was allocated to London Forest's Leyton garage, operating in an all-white livery complete with red bands and London Forest fleet names. The second was TPL4 (G608SGU), a similar bodied Leyland Tiger coach. This was allocated to Selkent at Catford. A red livery relieved by a grey skirt was applied to this vehicle.

A second former London Country Bus Services Plaxton Paramount bodied Leyland Tiger was acquired by London Buses Limited in March 1990. TP2 (A131EPA) was added to the London Central fleet where it found a home at New Cross. It carried large London Central fleet names on its red-based livery.

London Forest was the recipient of a second Plaxton Paramount bodied Leyland Tiger coach in March. Numbered TPL5 (G601XMD), it joined TPL3 at Leyton garage, receiving a similar livery.

London Coaches took stock of the remaining deliveries during 1990, all being allocated to Wandsworth. Nine arrived in April, all based on the DAF SB2305 chassis. Four of these, DD1 to DD4 (G901-4MCX), carried Duple 320 bodywork. The other five were all bodied by Van Hool. These were numbered DV62 to DV66 and were registered G962-6KJX.

A further seven second-hand coaches were taken into stock by London Coaches over the summer of 1990. Duple Laser bodied Volvo B10M RMU967Y and Plaxton Paramount 3200 bodied Volvo B10M were both acquired from Digby Stewart School of Roehampton in May. They were joined by Duple bodied DAF MB230 DD42 (E342EVH) which came on lease from the Stanley Hughes Group. From the same source came Duple 340 bodied DAF MB230s DD91 to DD93 (D291-3WCX). This had previously operated with London Coaches as DD1-3.

The final coach to be acquired in 1990 arrived at Wandsworth in July. DS3 (KJF300V) was a Duple bodied Volvo B58 coach. It was used by London Coaches as a driver training vehicle in a blue and white livery.

1991 was a slightly quieter year for the intake of coaches by London Buses and London Coaches. The first two arrived in February from the Stanley Hughes Group. DP86 (D286XCX) was a Plaxton bodied DAF; whilst E771WSV was a Duple 340 bodied Leyland Tiger which was not allocated a rolling stock number.

A pair of Plaxton Paramount bodied Leyland Tigers joined similar coaches at London Forest's Leyton garage in April. These were numbered TPL7 and TPL8 (G642/3GRO) and wore a white-based livery complete with red London Forest logos.

London Coaches also took stock of a fleet of coaches in April. The Van Hool Alizee bodied DAF SB2300 coaches wore an all-red livery and carried registration marks H523/4/6-9/31YCX, taking up fleet numbers DV24/6-9/31

A more unusual coach arrived with London Northern at Holloway in May. SKY1 (E469YWJ) was a tri-axle double-deck Auwarter Neoplan Skyliner. New in 1988 it was acquired from Coach Europe

Ltd. At this time, Holloway became the home to London Northern's small coaching fleet.

Duple bodied Volvo B58 YTA612S was added to the Westlink fleet in June 1991. Allocated to Hounslow Heath was also used by the company on private hire work.

London Coaches established an outstation in Northfleet in June, where thirty-two of the company's coaches were allocated. By the end of the month LD1/2, DD1-4, DV1-6, 8-19, 21/2, 55-8, 62/3 were generally operated from this new base.

DS1 and DS2 gained an all-over white livery in the summer of 1991.

1992 opened with the arrival of two Plaxton bodied DAF SB2305 coaches with London Buses Limited. DD35 and DD36 (J35/6GCX) were allocated to Plumstead when they arrived in January wearing a grey livery with a thin red skirt, complete with Selkent Travel fleet names. Van Hool bodied DAF DV67 (E648NCX) was also allocated to Plumstead, arriving with London Buses Limited in March. It was also put to use on private hire duties. A second coach arrived in March, this time being allocated to Edgware. Duple Dominant bodied Leyland Leopard LD5 (WGV867X) was leased from Kirkby Bus & Coach wearing an all-white livery. From the same source came TPL9 (D602MVR), a Plaxton Paramount 3200 bodied Leyland Tiger. The latter coach wore a white livery, relieved by a blue and red stripe.

The London Coaches operation was sold to its management in May 1992. This included the garage at Wandsworth and the outstation at Northfleet. Along with this was the fleet of sightseeing buses and the coaches used on commuter services. The coaches that transferred to the new company were LD1/2, DS1-3, DD1-3, DP86, DD92, DV1-24/6-9, 31, 55-60/2-6.

London Buses took stock of a Plaxton Paramount bodied DAF MB230 coach numbered DP1 (F637OHD). Arriving in August 1992 it was allocated to Plumstead.

The intake of coaches for 1993 totalled seven, with four of these being allocated to Selkent at Plumstead; two to Metroline at Cricklewood and the final example being allocated to London Northern at Holloway.

The quartet allocated to Plumstead were leased from the Stanley Hughes Group. These were Van Hool bodied DAF MB230 registered K536-9RJX, taking fleet numbers DV36 to DV39.

The pair of coaches allocated to Cricklewood were new to Shearings in 1990. Registered F789/91GNA, the pair of Duple 320 bodied Leyland Tigers were numbered TDL1 and TDL2 and were taken into stock during March 1993. VP1 (G91RGG), a Plaxton Paramount 3200 bodied Volvo B10M, new to Parks of Hamilton in 1990, arrived at the same time, being allocated to Holloway.

The opening months of 1994 saw five coaches re-registered by London Buses. In January, SKY1 gained new registration mark NDZ7937. In February, another four coaches gained new registration marks. LP5 and LP6 became 185CLT and 205CLT; VP1 took up new registration mark NDZ7936, whilst LD5 became 585CLT.

TPL5 and TPL7 were repainted into a silver and red livery in April of the same year.

Two second-hand coaches were acquired by London Buses in the first half of 1994. VP2 (F24HGG), a Plaxton Paramount 3200 bodied Volvo B10M was allocated to East London at North Street, Romford for private hire work in April.

VP3 (H637UWR), a Plaxton Paramount 3500 bodied Volvo B10M arrived in June. This was allocated to Metroline at Cricklewood.

Leaside Travel's TPL2 was involved in an accident on the M4 on 14 June 1994. A Plaxton Paramount 3500 bodied Volvo B10M coach was taken on loan between 20 June and 20 July at Stamford Hill to cover the loss of TPL2.

The various operations of London Buses Limited were privatised between September 1994 and January 1995. The coaching fleet was sold to the various operations, details of which vehicles went where is covered under the relevant company mentioned below.

Berkhof bodied DAF MB200 B593XNO was lent to London Transport for use on the Tours and Charter service in 1984. It is seen attending the Brighton Coach Rally 1985. *Gary Seamarks*

Four MCW Metroliners were purchased by London Coaches for use on their London to Birmingham Londonliner service. The first of these, ML1 (C101DYE) is seen on Park Lane heading towards the latter destination. *Gary Seamarks*

The original coach of choice was the Duple bodied DAF coach, the first of which arrived in 1986. DD2 (D292XCX) was delivered to London Coaches in 1987 and is seen parked at the St Paul's Cathedral coach park which is no longer in existence. *Gary Seamarks*

***Above*: In May** 1987 the Duple Dominant bodied AEC Reliance AD1 (AHE996T) arrived. It is seen above wearing full London Coaches livery. *Gary Seamarks*

***Below*: Three Van** Hool bodied DAF SB2305 coaches arrived in September 1987. DV3 (E313EVH) was the last of the trio and is seen keeping company with DV4 (E604LVH) outside Wandsworth garage. *David Haig*

Above: **LD4 (OMA504V)** was one of two Duple Dominant bodied Leyland Leopards that were acquired by London Buses in 1988. LD4 was allocated to the Bexleybus operation and painted blue and cream as seen above. *Phil Hambling*

Below: **LP5 arrived** with London Buses in 1989 from Cambus. Allocated to the Leaside operation, it gained cherished registration mark 185CLT in 1994. *Colin Lloyd*

***Above*: Later in** the year, Leaside were allocated a pair of Plaxton Paramount bodied Leyland Tiger coaches. TPL1 (G661WMD) was one of these smart coaches. *Colin Lloyd*

***Below*: Duple bodied** Volvo B58 YTA612S arrived in June 1991 and was used for both private hire and driver training work. *Colin Lloyd*

Above: **VP1 (G91RGG)** was the first of two Plaxton Paramount bodied Volvo B10M coaches taken into stock by London Buses Limited in 1990. VP1 was allocated to London Northern and is seen at Marble Arch. *Gary Seamarks*

Below: **Sister vehicle** VP2 (F24HGG) found itself allocated to North Street, Romford, where it was used in the East London Coaches fleet. It is seen out of service at the North Street garage. *Colin Lloyd*

GO-AHEAD LONDON

London Central took stock of a Plaxton Paramount bodied Leyland Tiger from fellow Go-Ahead company Voyager. Registered PCN762 it took fleet number TPL10 when it arrived in April 1995 and in October of the same year TPL10 was re-registered VLT71. In February 1997 TPL10 transferred from London Central to London General at Sutton. From here it was used on Surrey County Council school service 540 in the Redhill area.

London hosted the 2012 Olympic Games which required a large bus and coach operation. Whilst Stagecoach and First Group operated the majority of services required, Go-Ahead London operated just under 100 buses and coaches on various contracts. The coaches were taken on loan from other Go-Ahead companies. Brighton & Hove provided seven Scania coaches. Three of these were Irizar Century bodied Scania K114EBs which carried fleet numbers 501, 509 and 510 (YN08JAU, YN04ANU and YN05GZS). The other four also carried Irizar Century bodywork, these being based on Scania K340EB4 chassis. These were numbered 502 to 505 and carried registration marks HG08UHT, YR58RUH/U and UK59BCL. Go South Coast provided three Plaxton Paragon bodied Volvo B12M coaches. These were numbered 7084/5 and 7096 (WKZ8689, 8697, PX03KCN).

The final eighteen coaches to operate Olympic contracts were sourced from the Oxford Bus Company. Six of these were Jonckheere bodied Volvo B12Bs. These carried registration marks OA, OB, OC, OD, OE, OF02OXF and were numbered 29 to 34 in the Oxford fleet. The other twelve were Irizar Century bodied Scania K114EBs numbered 35 to 46. These were registered OW03LFP/R/L/S/X/K/N, AF, BF, CF, DF, EF53OXF.

Four coaches were taken into stock by Go-Ahead London in the opening months of 2015 for use in the commercial service fleet. UK05BCL, a Plaxton Panther bodied Volvo B12B, was first to arrive in January, taking up rolling stock number VC3. This coach was acquired from Tellings-Golden Miller. Two more similar coaches arrived in February registered NX51/52AAA, these becoming VC1 and VC2 in the Go-Ahead London fleet. The pair had previously operated with South Gloucestershire Bus Co., Patchway. VC4 (SF05XEC) also arrived in February. Acquired from Pikes of Andover, this was a Jonckheere Mistral bodied Volvo B12M. All four were used on rail replacement services, with VC1 and VC2 allocated to Northumberland Park and VC3 and VC4 to Luton. They were repainted into a pale cream livery relieved by a purple relief band and gold fleet names and numbers. In November 2015 VC1/2 moved from Northumberland Park to Croydon.

In November another two Plaxton Panther bodied Volvo B12B coaches arrived. VC5 (LK53KYZ) was acquired from Arriva Bus & Coach, whilst VC6 (L700SGB) was another to be acquired from the South Gloucestershire Bus & Coach Co. Ltd of Patchway. These were again allocated to the commercial service fleet.

VC1, VC2 and VC6 all lost their private registration marks during 2016. VC1 and VC2 gained their previous registration marks LK53KVY and LK53KWE in February; whilst VC6 regained its original mark, YN55WSV, in July.

VC1 moved from Croydon to Sittingbourne in January 2018, with VC2 moving from Croydon to Northumberland Park at the same time, both continuing to be used on rail replacement work.

The annual Wimbledon Tennis tournament needed three Jonckheere bodied Volvo B9R coaches to be lent to London General in July 2018 for the duration of the tournament. These coaches were registered PO12JNF, PO12JNK and PE13HCJ.

Three more second-hand coaches entered the Go-Ahead London fleet in March 2019 from sister Go-Ahead company East Yorkshire Motor Services. These took fleet numbers VC7 to VC9 (FN62CEA, CEU, YY63OEK). These Caetano Levante bodied Volvo B9Rs were received by the company in National Express livery, being repainted into the commercial services livery mentioned above before entering service. They were initially allocated to Northumberland Park, before moving to Luton in May 2019. It was at this time that Go-Ahead London had gained a long-term rail replacement contract between Stevenage and Hertford North, using coaches from the Luton allocation.

VC6 was lent to Brighton & Hove for a week at the end of November, beginning of December 2019 for use on rail replacement work.

Another four Caetano Levante bodied Volvo B9Rs were acquired from Go North East in October 2020. These continued the fleet number sequence, becoming VC10 to VC13 (FJ61GZC, FJ60HYB, FJ60KVM, FJ60KVO). They were officially allocated to Luton, and like the others being used on rail replacement work. However, these were outstationed in the Norfolk town of Kings Lynn.

VC6 was sold by the company during May 2021.

A year and a half after being acquired, VC11 and VC12 were repainted into the cream and burgundy commercial services livery in March 2022.

Brighton & Hove's 502 (HF08UHT), a Irizar PB bodied Scania K340EB4, was lent to Go-Ahead London for use on London 2012 Olympic Games contracts. It is photographed about to pass the Eaton Manor Transport Hub. *Gary Seamarks*

Twelve Irizar Century bodied Scania K114EBs were also used by Go-Ahead London, these originating with the Oxford Bus Company. OW03LFL is seen at Tower Hill whilst on Olympic duties. *Gary Seamarks*

In May 2023 Luton garage closed, VC7-9 at this time transferring to a new outstation established in the Bedfordshire town of Leighton Buzzard. VC10-3 transferred from the Kings Lynn outstation to Leighton Buzzard in December.

Go-Ahead London withdrew its fleet of coaches in June 2024. VC7, VC10-3 passed on to sister company Brighton & Hove; whilst VC8 and VC9 also passed to another Go-Ahead Group company, this being Dartline.

Right**: Bedford railway** station finds VC1 (LK53KVZ) and VC4 (SF05XEC) showing the difference between the Plaxton Panther (VC1) and Jonckheere Mistral (VC4). *Ben Everitt*

Below**: A sunny** Luton Transport Interchange finds VC8 (FN62CEU). VC8 was transferred to Go-Ahead London from sister Go-Ahead company East Yorkshire Motor Services in March 2019. It is seen operating a rail replacement journey to nearby Luton Airport Parkway. *Liam Farrer-Beddall*

LONDON NORTHERN

London Northern was privatised on 26 October 1994, with the lease of two coaches, Volvo B10M VP1 and Neoplan Skyliner SKY1, both of which were allocated to Holloway, passing to the new operator.

Three Van Hool Alizee coaches were acquired by London Northern in March 1995. VH1 (804DYE – originally F967GMW), was acquired from Silver Knight of Chippenham, via dealer Stuart Johnson. The second became VH2 (NJI9479). This was based on a DAF MB230 chassis, acquired from Carlton PSV. The third example was also based on the DAF MB230 chassis. It was registered G260EHD and took up stock number VH3, being acquired from Yeates. Both VH2 and VH3 were downseated from fifty-one-seaters to forty-nine-seaters before entering service. VH3 was also re-registered 283CLT. They wore a basic white livery, complete with a red skirt and turquoise band. They carried Sightseers logos along with London Northern fleet names. They were joined by a fourth Van Hool Alizee coach in April, this being fitted to a Volvo B10M chassis. VH4 (HIL6975) was acquired from Astra Travel of Harrogate and was also repainted into Sightseers livery. All four were allocated to Holloway garage.

MTL London Northern acquired the business of R&I Tours on 24 October 1995. Alongside the bus operation, a fleet of coaches were acquired, these are listed below:

> Iveco 35.8/Elme 44 (C843KGK); Iveco 35.6/Devon Conversion 58 (E783MLB); Toyota Coaster/Caetano Optimo 61 (E782MLB), 92 (WPX448), 94 (672DYA); Mercdes-Benz 811D/Optare StarRider 67 (UIL897), OM93 (165BXP); Ford Transit/Chassis Developments 77 (C945FMJ); Kassbhorer Optimo S81-3 (RIB6197-9); Kassbhorer Rational 901 (RIB6195); Mercedes-Benz 811D/Robin Hood 87/90 F87/90GGC; Mercedes-Benz 609D/Robin Hood 303 (D85DOT); Volvo B10M/Plaxton Paramount 3500 VP330/3/4/6/7/8/41 (SVO89, 43FJF, RIB5084/6, 7017/8,

OO1942); LAG Panoramic 342 (RIB4315); Fiat 59.12/Cacciamalli 343/4 (N713/4FLN) and Mercedes-Benz 814D/Cacciamalli MC345-7 (N715-7FLN).

London Northern purchased two Van Hool Alizee bodied Volvo B10M coaches in 1996, these arriving in June. Registered N655/6EWJ, they were numbered VH5 and VH6 respectively. A month later, in July, a pair of Caetano bodied Toyota H2B50R coaches were taken into stock. These carried registration marks N781/2SJU and were numbered TC10 and TC11 by the company. The pair were allocated to North Acton, with three more Van Hool Alizee bodied Volvo B10M coaches taken into stock in July. These followed on from the June deliveries as VH7 to VH9 (N657-9EWJ).

MTL London Northern was acquired by Metroline on 17 August 1998. A number of the coaches passed to the new owner.

METROLINE

Metroline was privatised on 7 October 1995, with four coaches passing to the new operator. These were Leyland Leopard LD5, Leyland Tigers TDL1 and TDL2, and Volvo B10M VP3. All four were allocated to the commercial service fleet which was based at Cricklewood.

TDL1/2 and VP3 were returned to Yeates of Loughborough in June 1995.

In April 1995 a pair of Plaxton Premiere 320 bodied Dennis Javelins arrived. Numbered DP1 and DP2 (K260/1FUV) these also joined the commercial service fleet. These had formerly operated with London-based coach operator Redwings.

Metroline acquired the business of Brents Coaches of Watford on 10 October 1995. This brought a large number of coaches into the fleet. Following the acquisition of Brents, the commercial services along with three coaches transferred to Watford from Cricklewood, with the Brents operation becoming responsible for private hire and excursion work. The vehicles acquired were as follows:

> DAF MB230/Plaxton Paramount 3500 (E647RCX, E64SJS); Mercedes-Benz 408D/Whittaker (7804PP); Leyland Tiger/Plaxton Paramount 3500 (H23/4JMJ); Mercedes-Benz 814D/Plaxton Beaver (K337ABH); Mercedes-Benz 811D/Optare StarRider (G732BVS, K318FYG); Mercedes-Benz 410D/Autobus Classique (K712/20GBE, M840MEE); DAF MB230/Van Hool Alizee (K108TCP, L513EHD, M626RCP); Mercedes-Benz 811D/Autobus Classique (L959JFU, M633/4UCT); Mercedes-Benz 814D/Optare StarRider (L671PWT); Dennis Javelin/Plaxton Premiere 320 (N464BHE, N10, 20JET); Leyland Leopard/Duple Dominant III (YLU910X); DAF SB230/Plaxton Paramount 3200 (A991JJU, C461JCP); Volvo B10M/Plaxton Paramount 3200 (B862/9XYR, C513/8DND) and DAF MB230/Plaxton Paramount 3200 (D542GFH, D353RCY).

Metroline updated some of the rolling stock in the Brents fleet in 1996, taking eight coaches into stock in April and May. April saw two new Autobus Classique bodied coaches entered the fleet. N980WJL was based on a Mercedes-Benz 711D chassis, whilst N989AEF was an example of a Mercedes-Benz 814D. The other six all arrived in May. Two of these were Autobus bodied 814Ds registered N330BAJ and N979WJL, with four Plaxton Premiere 350 bodied Volvo B10Ms (N963-6DWJ) completing delivery of the eight.

These were complemented by three Van Hool bodied DAF coaches. L536WHD and M609RCP were based on the SB3000 chassis; whilst G971KJX was a MB230 model; the latter being sourced from Scorpo Travel of Gosport.

The arrival of the new coaches saw DP1, DP2 and H23/4JMJ return off-lease.

Leyland Leopard LD5 (585CLT) was re-registered YLX410X in January 1997.

The Watford base of Brents Coaches was closed in January 1998, transferring to Metroline's Harlesden garage.

Metroline's coaching operations were expanded on 17 August 1998 when the operations of MTL London Northern were acquired, this including some coaches from the former R&I Tours operations. The new operation traded as Metroline London Northern Ltd.

A pair of former Stagecoach Glasgow Caetano bodied Dennis Javelin coaches were acquired for use with the Brents fleet. These fifty-three coaches carried registration marks P771/9BJF.

During 1999, the Brents Coaches operations closed down.

The Comfort-Delgro Group ventured into a new coach operation in November 2015 when Braddell Ltd commenced a service between London St Pancras International and Stansted Airport. Ten Mercedes-Benz Tourismo coaches were purchased by the company, these being maintained by Metroline at Perivale. Numbered MBT1 to MBT10 (BG65VXA-F/H/J/K/L) wore a blue and yellow livery similar to that worn by Scottish Citylink coaches. The route was numbered 767. Before these coaches arrived, a number of coaches were hired from various sources. Four Plaxton bodied Volvo B12B coaches came from Hamilton Grey, these being registered HIG5338/9/44/5 and MIL6683. A pair of Plaxton Panther bodied Volvo B12BTs registered SF07ANX and SP07CAA were sourced from New Adventure Travel of Cardiff. YJ08EAC, a Van Hool TD921, was lent to the company from the Howard Travel Group of Great Sankey. A solitary Van Hool TDX21 registered 142-G-6 was loaned from Cullinan of Galway. These were returned once the new coaches entered service. The service proved popular but suddenly ceased on the 28 October 2017. After initial storage at Hayes, the coaches were redistributed, with some of them moving to sister Comfort-Delgro operation Westbus.

Above: **LD5 (585CLT)** passed to Metroline at the time of privatisation. It is seen whilst still under London Buses Limited ownership, having just passed Victoria Coach Station. *Colin Lloyd*

Below: **Callinan Coaches** was owned by the Comfort-Delgro Group, the parent company of Metroline. In 2015 the company set up an express service between St Pancras International and Stansted Airport, branded as the Stansted Citylink. BG65VXD was one of ten Mercedes-Benz Tourismo coaches used on the service. Maintenance was carried out by Metroline. St Pancras International provides the backdrop to this photograph. *Liam Farrer-Beddall*

LEASIDE BUSES/ARRIVA LONDON

Leaside Buses was privatised on 29 September 1994 with five coaches passing to the new company. These were Leyland Leopards LP5 and LP6 (185CLT, 205CLT) and Leyland Tigers TPL1, 2 and 8 (G661/2WMD, H643GRO). All five were added to the Leaside Travel operation based at Stamford Hill. July 1995 saw TPL2 experience engine problems. Van Hool Alizee bodied Volvo B10M E904MUC was loaned from sister company Grey-Green to cover whilst TPL2 was repaired. A month later, in August, TPL1 and TPL2 gained new cherished registration marks 124CLT and 361CLT.

Two Duple 320 bodied Volvo B10M coaches were acquired from Grey-Green in 1996. Registered E892/3KYW, the pair took up stock numbers DV1 and DV2. Again, these were allocated to Stamford Hill for use in the Leaside Travel fleet. By April the pair had gained new registrations 185CLT and 205CLT.

In April 1996, two Plaxton Premiere 350 bodied DAF SB3000 coaches arrived from Hughes DAF of Cleckheaton. DP1 and DP2 (N551/2LUA) wore an all-white livery, relieved by Leaside Travel fleet names. These replaced Leyland Leopards LP5 and LP6 in April, these being re-registered FYT335/6V during the month, the pair passing to County Bus & Coach during the same month.

A third Plaxton Premiere 350 bodied DAF SB3000 coach was taken into stock by Leaside in March 1997. This followed on as DP3 and was registered P753RWU. At the same time DV1 and DV2 left the fleet, passing to County Bus & Coach. Their place being taken by a pair of Plaxton Paramount bodied Volvo B10M coaches, VPL1/2 (C874/6CYX), both being sourced from Grey-Green. Stamford Hill was again the recipient of these coaches.

A fourth new coach arrived in June 1997. This time an Ikarus bodied DAF SB3000 was chosen, taking up rolling stock number DI4 (P754RWU).

A re-organisation within the Cowie Group saw the Leaside Travel fleet transfer from Leaside Buses to County Bus & Coach on 27 October 1997, the coaches moving into the latter operator's garage at Edmonton. DI4, DP1-3, TPL1/2/8 and VPL1/2 made the move.

However, another re-organisation in 1998 saw the County Bus & Coach operation based at Edmonton transfer to Arriva London North, the Leaside Travel operation passing back to Leaside from 3 October. TPL1/2/8, DP1-3, DI4 and VPL1/2 all returned. By this time DP1-3 and DI4 had been renumbered DPL551-3, DI554 and VPL1/2 were renumbered VPL3 and VPL4 respectively. In addition, five other coaches were also transferred. These were Plaxton Paramount bodied Leyland Tiger TPL518 (530MUY); a solitary Duple bodied Leyland Tiger registered C254SPC, this becoming TDL54. A pair of Bova Futuras registered G545JOG and JIW3696 were numbered BOV595 and BOV596. The final coach was a Plaxton Paramount bodied Volvo B10M numbered VPL503 (H903AHS). The pair of Bovas did not last long, departing the fleet in the first part of 1999.

1998 concluded with the arrival of four Van Hool Alizee bodied DAF MB230s from Arriva London North East, the new name for Grey-Green. Registered G905-8TYR these were allotted fleet numbers DVH5 to DVH8, these being allocated to Edmonton.

In August 1999, Volvo B10M VPL503 (H803AHS) gained new registration mark VLT32; with DPL2 (N552LUA), following suit in July 2000, becoming 398CLT.

Two second-hand coaches were added to the Leaside Travel fleet in March 2001. DP5 (R162GNW) was a Plaxton Excalibur bodied DAF SB3000. It was joined by Plaxton Premiere bodied DAF SB3000 DP6 (T56AUA).

In December 2003 seven coaches were re-registered. DI4/5 became 480CLT and 519CLT; DPL1 took new registration mark 217CLT. DP3 (P753RWU) was re-registered 319CLT, whilst DP6 (T56AUA) became 330CLT. The final pair were DVH6 and DVH8 which took cherished registration marks VLT27 and VLT47.

Ikarus Blue Danube bodied DAF SB3000 coach came south in May 2004 from Arriva Yorkshire. It became DI7 (T110AUA) in the Leaside Travel fleet.

In October 2005 three Volvo B10M coaches were re-registered when VPL3 and VPL4 became C874/6CYX, with VPL503 re-gaining its original registration mark H903AHS. The remaining coaches in the fleet (DI4/7, DP1-4/5/6, DVH6/8 and TPL1/2/8) re-gained their original registration marks in December, which also marked the end of the coaching operation with Leaside Buses, the coaches being sold to Ensign Bus during the month. The cherished registration marks carried by the coaches transferred to MA-class Mercedes-Benz Citaro Gs or VLW-class Volvo B7TLs.

STAGECOACH LONDON/EAST LONDON BUS GROUP

East London and Selkent were both purchased by the Stagecoach Group on 6 September 1994. Stagecoach inherited eleven coaches from London Buses Limited. Leyland Tigers TPL5 and TPL7, and Volvo B10M VP2 passed to Stagecoach East London, the three being allocated to North Street, Romford. Stagecoach Selkent took stock of the other eight coaches. These were DAFs DD35 and DD36; DP1 and DV36-9, 67. These were allocated to Plumstead for private hire work.

The first coach to be acquired by Stagecoach London from within the Stagecoach empire arrived in March 1995. WGB834W, a Duple Dominant IV bodied Volvo B10M, was acquired from Stagecoach Western Scottish. It was repainted into standard white with stripes livery at Carlisle before travelling to London. It was allocated to Plumstead, where it was used as a driver training vehicle. It was originally numbered 3010, being renumbered 3007 soon after. It remained in London for three months, passing to Stagecoach South Coast Buses in June 1995. The same month saw TPL5 (G601XMD) also depart the fleet.

Three Plaxton Paramount 3500 bodied Volvo B10M coaches were acquired by Stagecoach East London in September 1995. VP4/5/7

(H654/5/7UWR) originated with Wallace Arnold, being sourced from Kirkby Bus & Coach. Allocated to North Street, Romford they allowed TPL7 and VP2/3 to return off lease. In July 1998, VP4/5/7 were re-registered 630DYE, WLT890 and WLT898. These were also repainted at the same time.

The first of three Plaxton Premiere Interurban bodied Dennis Javelin coaches arrived in April 1999 registered M105CCD. It was joined in June by two more registered M106/8CCD. Acquired from Stagecoach South they were numbered J5, J6 and J8. The trio were allocated to North Street, Romford where they were used to replace older rolling stock in the private hire fleet. J5 was repainted red, whilst the other two initially wore the Stagecoach stripe livery.

A problem with parking space at Romford in 2000 saw VP4/5 and J5/6/8 transfer to Barking. The latter three coaches were cascaded to Stagecoach Devon in March 2001. They were replaced by three Plaxton Premiere bodied Volvo B10Ms in April 2001, these arriving from Stagecoach Devon. These coaches were registered CSU992, SYC852 and CSU978, taking up fleet numbers VP6 to VP8. These also found a home at Barking. The Stagecoach provincial stripe livery was worn by these coaches.

VP4 and VP5 were replaced by a pair of well-travelled Jonckheere Deauville bodied Volvo B10M coaches sourced from Stagecoach East. L157/8LBW took up rolling stock numbers VJ4 and VJ5 with Stagecoach London. They arrived carrying Stagecoach Air Express livery before being Repainted. Carrying the fleet numbers mentioned, Stagecoach referred to the pair as VJ8 and VJ9. Both entered service from North Street, Romford.

Stagecoach renumbered its fleet on 1 January 2003 into a single five-digit system, removing any duplications with in its various operations, making it easier to transfer buses and coaches. The four coaches operating in London at this time (VP6/7 and VJ8/9) became 52219, 52217, 52023 and 52022.

Stagecoach London were allocated a handful of workings on the Megabus.com network in 2004, using a fleet of Leyland Olympians. In February 2005 a double-deck Neoplan Skyliner was briefly loaned from Stagecoach Bluebird, the coach in question was numbered 50128 (SV54ELJ). March 2005 saw three similar double-deck coaches allocated to the London operation. 50136 to 50138 (LX05BWL/M/N) were allocated to Leyton garage, replacing Leyland Olympians that had originally been used. Two more, 50139/40, had also been earmarked for London but were diverted elsewhere within the Stagecoach group. 50138 departed the fleet in November 2005.

The first of three Jonckheere Mistral bodied Volvo B10M coaches were added to the private hire fleet in November 2005. 52604 (S134KRM) was acquired from Stagecoach Midlands. It was joined by similar 52615 and 52616 (S905/6JHG) in January 2006. These were quickly repainted out of National Express livery, receiving an all-red livery relieved by a blue skirt. 52617 (S457BCE) and 52623 (S903CCD) were also acquired, this time from Stagecoach North West, in December 2005 (52617) and January 2006 (52623). These latter two coaches were used on the Megabus.com network.

52022/3 passed to Stagecoach North West in June 2006; with 52617 and 52623 moving to Stagecoach Midland Red South in May 2006.

On 23 June 2006 Stagecoach sold East London and Selkent to the Australian Bank Macquarie, who renamed the operations the East London Bus Group. 52217/9, 52604/15/6 were transferred to the newly formed company.

In January 2007 Plaxton bodied Volvo B10Ms 52217/9 (SYC852, CSU992) were re-registered back to their original registration marks (M407/9BFG).

The East London Coaches private hire fleet was closed on 2 February 2007. It was at this time that 52217/9 and 52604/15/6 were sold to Ensign Bus.

A pair of Plaxton bodied Volvo B10M coaches were acquired from Stagecoach Manchester in late 2008. 52248 (M948TSX) and 52296

(N446XVA) were allocated to Rainham where they were used as driver training coaches. Similar 52214 (M404BFG) was acquired from the same source in January 2009, also joining the other two at Rainham for use as a driver training coach. They had departed the Stagecoach London fleet by April 2011.

***Above*: Three Plaxton** bodied Dennis Javelin coaches arrived in April 1999 from Stagecoach Devon. The first numerically was J5 (M105CCD), and is seen at the Showbus rally at the Imperial War Museum, Duxford showing the gold fleet names applied to these coaches. *Gary Seamarks*

***Opposite top*: Originally numbered** VP6, CSU992 was later renumbered 52219 by Stagecoach London. This Plaxton bodied Volvo B10M is seen operating a private hire contract, mingling with other provincial Stagecoach buses as it departs Bedford bus station. *David Beddall*

Opposite bottom: Three Neoplan Skyliner double-deck coaches were briefly allocated to Stagecoach London's Leyton garage for use on the megabus.com network of express services. The last of these was 50138 (LX05BWN) which is seen attending the 2005 Waterden Road, Stratford garage open day. *David Beddall*

East London Coaches
52219
East London Coaches
52219
Stagecoach
VP6
CSU 992

low cost inter city travel
megabus.com
megabus.com
50138
LX05 BWN

CAPITAL CITYBUS

Capital Citybus operated a solitary coach. 945 (REA945W) was a Plaxton Supreme bodied Bedford acquired by the company in October 1996. It was used as a driver training coach.

LONDON UNITED

Unlike other former London Buses Limited divisions, London United never inherited any coaches. It wasn't until May 1998 that any coaches were operated. Two Van Hool Alizee bodied DAF coaches registered K532/4RJX were taken into stock at the company's West Ramp, Heathrow base. They were returned off lease in October 1998.

It wasn't until 2011 that any more coaches entered the London United fleet. The first of two Plaxton Paragon bodied Volvo B12B coaches was acquired from sister RATP Group company Yellow Buses of Bournemouth in August. Carrying registration mark HF53OBH it took up stock number VB1. HF53OBG followed in November, being numbered VB2 by the company. Both were allocated to Fulwell where they were used in the commercial services fleet.

Between December 2014 and January 2016, fourteen Caetano Levante coaches were acquired by the RATP Group for use with London United. The first pair were based on the Scania K340EB4 chassis. FJ09DXP and FJ09DXR arrived in December 2014. Numbered SL1 and SL2 by the company they were allocated to Twickenham for the commercial fleet, this being named United Motorcoaches. These coaches were acquired from Tellings-Golden Miller.

The next seven arrived in July 2015 from Yourbus, Heanor. These Caetano Levante bodied Volvo B9Rswere registered FJ11GLY, MME/F/K/U, MLY and MOA, the seven coaches took stock numbers VL1 to VL7. VL1/3/4/7 wore National Express livery, whilst the other three wore an all-white livery. Like SL1 and SL2 they were allocated to the commercial services fleet, this time at Twickenham. They were used by London United on some workings on National Express services A1, A4 and A6, these connecting London Victoria with Luton, Gatwick and Stansted Airports. An eighth B9R arrived in August 2015, this time from Selwyns of Runcorn. It followed on as VL8 (FJ56PBF), joining the others on National Express work. It was destroyed by fire on 26 March 2016 whilst at Stansted Airport.

Four additional Caetano Levante bodied Scania K340EB4 coaches were acquired from Selwyns in January 2016. These were numbered SL3 to SL6 and carried registration marks FJ58AJU/V and FJ59APX/Y. They were added to the United Motorcoaches fleet at Twickenham.

The RATP Group renumbered London United and London Sovereign into a single five-digit fleet numbering sequence in March 2016. The coaches were renumbered VB60001/2 (VB1/2); VL65001-8 (VL1-8) and SL65009-14 (SL1-6). In May, VB60001/2 were renumbered 65011/2, meaning that SL3-6 became SL65013-6.

The majority of the coaching fleet was sold to Ensign Bus in January 2019. VB65012 was last to leave, doing so in October 2019.

FIRST CENTREWEST/FIRST CAPITAL

First London's first experience of operating coaches came in June 1998 when a Caetano Optimo III bodied Toyota Coaster registered M582DAF was lent to Centrewest at Westbourne Park. It was loaned from Western National, retaining its owner's fleet number (582). The coach was used as a standby vehicle, shuttling patrons of the Metropole Hotel. It returned to Western National in July.

First Capital began to amass a fleet of coaches for use on rail replacement work, these being based at Rainham. The first arrived in February 2005 in the form of a Plaxton bodied Dennis Javelin. Acquired from First Berkshire it carried fleet number DC21090 (M290FAE). It was joined by two similar coaches in November, these taking stock numbers DC21121/2 (N821/2KWS). A month later, in December, these were transferred to Dagenham.

Three Plaxton Excalibur bodied Volvo B12T coaches arrived from First Coaches Ltd of Bristol in April 2007. VCT20201-3 (T701-3JLD) were also allocated to Dagenham for use on both private hire and rail replacement work. In August 2007 they were on long-term loan to sister company First Essex Buses, also for use on rail replacement work. These returned in 2008. VCT20202 then went on loan to First Berkshire at Bracknell in October 2008.

21090, 21121/2 departed the fleet in February 2009.

SCF64791-4/8 (133CLT, M792TCF, 503CLT, WLT659, 811DYE) entered the fleet in August 2009. These were allocated to the training fleet based at Dagenham, being acquired from First Berkshire. They remained in the fleet until April 2011 when they were sold on for further use.

These coaches were re-registered to M791/3/4TCF and N798WAN in July 2010 and in October VCT20201 was placed on loan with First Berkshire at Bracknell, returning to First London in December.

First London closed the majority of its operations in June 2013. The coaches were retained by First Capital until July, at which time they moved on to First Midlands at Worcester.

In 2011 the first coaches were allocated to the London United fleet. A pair of Volvo B12B coaches with Plaxton bodywork arrived for use in the commercial services fleet. VB1 (HF53OBH) is seen at the 2012 Fulwell garage open day, with VB2 parked behind. *Liam Farrer-Beddall*

***Above*: London United** won several National Express contracts in 2015 and took a fleet of eight Caetano Levante bodied Volvo B9R coaches. VL6 (FJ11MLY) is photographed rounding Hyde Park Corner wearing National Express logos. *Liam Farrer-Beddall*

***Below*: United Motorcoaches** was the name used by London United for its commercial fleet in the mid-2010s. January 2016 saw the arrival of FJ59APX, a Caetano Levante bodied Scania K340EB4, which was numbered SL65015 in March 2016, having originally been numbered SL5. It is seen wearing the United Motorcoach livery passing on the outskirts of Kempston, Bedfordshire. *Liam Farrer-Beddall*

SOURCES

Ian's Bus Stop: www.busspotter.com

Various issues of *The London Bus*; London Omnibus Traction Society

Lane, K; *An Illustrated History of London Buses*, Ian Allan Publishing, 1997